Care of
Souls
in the
Classic
Tradition

THOMAS C. ODEN

Care of Souls in the Classic Tradition

Don S. Browning, *editor*

THEOLOGY AND PASTORAL CARE

FORTRESS PRESS
PHILADELPHIA

For Edrita

without whose companionship I could not have
taken this journey

Biblical quotations, unless otherwise noted, are from The New English Bible, © The Delegates of the Oxford University Press and the
Syndics of the Cambridge University Press 1961, 1970. Reprinted by
permission.

Library of Congress Cataloging in Publication Data

Oden, Thomas C.
   Care of souls in the classic tradition.

   (Theology and pastoral care series)
   Bibliography: p.
   1. Pastoral counseling.   2. Pastoral theology.
   3. Gregory I, Pope, ca. 540–604.   I. Title.   II. Series.
   BV4012.2.3 1984   253.5   83-48912
   ISBN 0-8006-1729-0

K478L83   Printed in the United States of America   1–1729

Contents

Series Foreword

Our purpose in the Theology and Pastoral Care Series is to present ministers and church leaders with a series of readable books that will (1) retrieve the theological and ethical foundations of the Judeo-Christian tradition for pastoral care, (2) develop lines of communication between pastoral theology and the other disciplines of theology, (3) create an ecumenical dialogue on pastoral care, and (4) do this in such a way as to affirm yet go beyond the recent preoccupation of pastoral care with secular psychotherapy and the other social sciences.

The books in this series are written by authors who are well acquainted with psychology, psychotherapy, and the other social sciences. All of the authors affirm the importance of these disciplines for modern societies and for ministry in particular, but they see them also as potentially destructive of human values unless they are guided in their practical application by tested religious and ethical traditions. But to retrieve the best of the Judeo-Christian tradition for the church's care and counseling is a challenging intellectual task—a task to which few writers in the area of pastoral care have attended with sufficient thoroughness. This series addresses that task out of a broad ecumenical stance, with all of the authors taking an ecumenical approach to theology. Besides a vigorous investigation of Protestant resources, there are specific treatments of pastoral care in Judaism and Catholicism.

We hope that the series will help ministers and church leaders view afresh the theological and ethical foundations of care and counseling. All of the books have a practical dimension, but even more important than that, they help us see care and counseling differently. Compared with writings of the last thirty years in this field, some of the books will seem startlingly different. They will need to be read and pondered with care. But I have little doubt that the series will make a profound and lasting impact upon the way we understand and practice our care for one another.

In *Care of Souls in the Classic Tradition*, Tom Oden continues an argument for which he has become widely known. For some years he has maintained that modern pastoral care should once again ground itself in the beliefs, moral assumptions, and practical sensibilities of the great ecumenical councils and major church fathers which he believes make up the consensus of the classical tradition. Oden is telling us that we should let the tradition—its central witness on a wide variety of issues—work for us. If we do this, certainly our theological and moral worlds will be more settled, but furthermore, we also will discover a rich treasure of concrete pastoral practices which we have all but ignored in the modern period.

Professor Oden chooses to illustrate his point by discussing the most influential single author on pastoral care in the history of the church—Gregory the Great, who was Bishop of Rome from A.D. 540–604. Gregory's *Book of Pastoral Rule* is the single most widely read book, outside of the Bible itself, ever written on the subject of pastoral care. As old as it is, Tom Oden helps us see it as a strangely modern book. By this he means that it anticipates much of what we value in contemporary theories without losing contact with the central witness of the Christian tradition. Gregory's *Rule* is sensitive to human differences, ethically serious without being moralistic, and, in its own way, psychologically dynamic. Oden claims that Gregory had deep insight into the polarities of different types of personal and spiritual distortions. In addition, he had great insight into what these polarities might mean for different approaches to care.

Tom Oden is one of our country's leading authors in the area of pastoral theology and the dialogue between theology and the social sciences. He is Henry Anson Butz Professor of Theology at the School of Theology, Drew University.

DON S. BROWNING

Preface

What curious fate has befallen the classical tradition of pastoral care in the last five decades? Positively, there has been a sustained attempt to listen intently to psychoanalysis and various psychotherapies. Their findings, approaches, and clinical resources have been received into contemporary pastoral practice. Negatively, there has been a pervasive amnesia toward the classical Christian past. This has resulted in a bland sense of absent-mindedness and a growing naiveté toward the wisdom of classical pastoral care.

Admittedly there are some exceptions (among whom Joachim Scharfenberg, Frank Lake, and Don Browning are the most significant). But as one looks over the key pastoral writers of the last half century, from Anton Boisen to the present, one wonders how it could have happened that despite our best intentions the classical pastoral tradition could have been so quickly misplaced and atrophied. Yet it is this very pragmatic, nonclassical (at times even polemically anticlassical) tradition of American pastoral care that is now being exported around the world, with Dietrich Stollberg, Heije Faber, Herman Andriessen, and others leading the way problematically toward the Americanization of pastoral care in Europe. Even the best representatives of American pastoral counseling such as Seward Hiltner, Howard Clinebell, and John Patton have not really probed the depths of the classical tradition except for occasional selective attention to it—as each one of them, I think, would readily acknowledge.

Our purpose here is to inquire into the theological and historical foundations of modern pastoral care. The fabric of effective pastoral work involves the constant interweaving of scriptural wisdom, historical awareness, constructive theological reasoning, situational discernment, and personal empathy. It is best studied by examining case materials of concrete problems of pastoral counsel, viewed in the light of scripture and tradition.

Within the confines of such a small book we cannot make such a detailed historical inquiry or theological investigation as would cover numerous figures or answer every objection. Therefore, we have focused upon a single pivotal representative of classical pastoral care, seeking to show the astonishing relevance of that one figure for ministry today.

Contemporary ministry does not have to look about frantically for untested models of integration of theology and pastoral care. For we already have several powerful models in the classical tradition of pastoral care. One might reasonably think of John Chrysostom, Ambrose, Augustine, Luther, Calvin, Baxter, Wesley, or Kierkegaard as a potential centerpiece for a discussion such as we here intend. But we have chosen that singular figure whose work has remained more quietly influential on the history of pastoral care than any other. Our key classic exemplar of pastoral integration is that remarkably effective Augustinian Bishop of Rome of the late sixth century, Gregory the Great (A.D. 540–604), who astutely gathered up the pastoral wisdom of the patristic period and energetically set in motion the basic direction of the medieval pastoral tradition.

We do not assume that the reader will already be thoroughly informed about Gregory, who remains a much neglected figure, ironically more neglected in our century than in any since his death. Few modern secondary treatises have dealt significantly with Gregory; even fewer are in English, and most of these are out of print. So the reader is easily forgiven if he or she expresses surprise or pleads ignorance. Gregory's writings have never been adequately translated into English.[1] This is one reason it is fitting now to reconstruct Gregory's contribution for modern readers. There remains a huge secondary literature on Augustine, Luther, Calvin, Loyola, and Wesley, all of whose influence on pastoral care was vast but arguably less universal than that of Gregory. For the whole millenium following his life, the one book that dominated pastoral theory and practice more than any other was Gregory's inimitable *Pastoral Care*.

Our purpose is not merely the veneration of longevity or the archaic exercise of excavating an ancient figure, however great. Rather, we intend to show the practical relevance of Gregory's pastoral care for the effective integration of theological and pastoral wisdom today.

In what follows we are trying to avoid three stumbling blocks: (1) an antihistorical view of pastoral theology; (2) an antipastoral approach to historical theology; and (3) an antitheological style of pastoral care. All three of these myopias fail to search for the necessary integration. Modern American pastoral work has been stronger in personal and practical aspects than in historical and theological awareness. We are seeking to develop a classical approach to the theology of pastoral care that will be practically useful to the working pastor. The constant interweaving of theological reflection and pastoral counsel may be viewed as we examine case materials of classical pastoral care.

Before launching into Gregory's work directly, we must address the present situation of pastoral care, showing how the wisdom of Gregory still addresses our modern discontents. In chapter 1 we will speak candidly of the deep trouble in which modern pastoral care now finds itself. To do so is to feel something like a physician speaking in solemn tones to the family of a gravely ill patient who knows nothing of the illness: the patient is amnesiac. We will offer a brief personal account of how we have come upon the scene of this dilemma. We will show the symptoms of this amnesia, letting readers judge for themselves concerning the seriousness of the illness. We will suggest reasons why pastoral counseling stands today in an unprecedented identity crisis.

In order to find our way back to the center of pastoral identity, we will tentatively accept Gregory as our guide and carefully follow and evaluate the direction in which he leads us. We will examine Gregory's pastoral method and show how he applies that method to various pastoral situations. We do not imply that Gregory is the only model. He may not even be the best model. But there is no doubt that he has been an exceptionally influential model who deserves a full reassessment.

Chapter 2 offers a brief biographical introduction to Gregory as pastor. We will not dwell long on the details of his life, however fascinating they may be, since our purpose is not historical description but pastoral-theological integration. We will set forth the crucial working assumptions underlying his pastoral theology. We will ask whether his work anticipates contemporary psychotherapies and how he would seek to prepare the soul guide for praxis.

All this is preparatory to the central concerns of chapters 3 and 4—an examination of Gregory's intriguing analysis of the varied ways in which contextual pastoral counseling responds variably to the special claims of persons in different, even opposite, situations. Gregory's sixth century pastoral method clearly anticipates modern case study methods, although with more emphasis on types of cases, arranged in polarities. Gregory presented these cases as a deliberate series of bipolar types to which every wise pastor, it is assumed, would learn to respond contextually. He set forth thirty-six of these polarities, analyzing seventy-two cases that require distinct sorts of pastoral wisdom. We will selectively review some of these prototype cases, concluding with an analysis of Gregory's penetrating reflections on providing pastoral care through preaching, centered on the problem of "contrary compulsions." This trajectory will provide us with a sustained view of a brilliant pastor at work showing others how the pastoral office impinges on pastoral tasks and how a wise contextual pastoral care finds its grounding in Scripture and church teaching.

Biblical quotations, unless otherwise noted, are from the New

English Bible. Unless otherwise noted, quotations from Gregory the Great are from the Henry Davis translation of Gregory, *Pastoral Care*, Ancient Christian Writers Series, vol. 11, Westminster, Md., Newman Press, 1950, subsequently republished by Paulist Press, hereafter noted as *PC*. If a quotation is taken from the earlier James Barmby translation, it will be marked *BPR*, for Gregory, *The Book of Pastoral Rule*, Nicene and Post-Nicene Fathers, (hereafter noted NPNF), 2d series, vol. 12, Grand Rapids, Mich.: Wm. B. Eerdmans, 1976. In either case, the reference will be by section number rather than page number, in order to serve the convenience of the reader who may have one translation available, but not another. Thus Book 1, section 3 will be noted as *PC*1. 3 (or if in the Barmby translation, as *BPR* 1. 3).

The core argument of chapter 1 was first presented as an address to the American Assocation of Pastoral Counselors at its national conference in Washington, D.C., 1979, and was presented in an amended form to the World Congress of Pastoral Care and Counseling in Edinburgh, 1979. It has appeared in a mutation in *The Journal of Pastoral Care*, vol. 34, March 1980. The most frequent response to these preliminary forms of the proposal has been this: It seems right and important that we recover the classical pastoral tradition now lost from active memory, but will you please give us some plausible example of classical pastoral care at work, so we can grasp its relevance for pastoral care today? This book attempts to answer that legitimate request.

Introduction

Before we ask "Gregory Who?" or "Why him?" it is first necessary to look candidly at the contemporary situation of pastoral care to ask why it needs ancient pastoral wisdom. Otherwise, we might give the skewed impression that we are merely reviewing Gregory as a historical exercise only, with no direct relevance to the pressing dilemmas of current pastoral care. To avoid this misunderstanding, we will take several careful steps to introduce ourselves properly to the issues that lie ahead.

We will first set forth a fundamental principle of theological dialogue with psychotherapy: The empathic acceptance that is implicitly presupposed in effective psychotherapy is made explicit in the Christian witness to revelation. This hypothesis, which we first stated over two decades ago, remains a key premise of the ensuing discussion.

It is appropriate to explain how I have journeyed from that preliminary hypothesis to the more vexing problems of this book. The argument could have been stated without any window at all into my own personal history. Yet it may be useful to show how and why I have now come full circle to a fundamentally revised set of questions and how they mesh with the present dilemmas of pastoral care. Every time I tell something of my personal story, I find to my amazement that others mention with great feeling that they too have experienced something analogous and that my story has helped them see what has happened to them.

From this autobiographical beginning point it becomes meaningful to take on the major technical issue of this chapter, asking whether pastoral counseling has a definable historic identity? Can we textually and historically define the central tradition of classical Christian pastoral care? A descriptive answer to this question will allow us better to ask about the ironic fate of that identity in our own time: How has historic pastoral care been remembered by us? Have we lost or misplaced that treasure in our modern broken vessels? Only then will our constructive question emerge with power: Can we recover that treasure? And if so, what is the promise of an enriched synthesis between classical and contemporary pastoral care? By the conclusion of the first chapter we will begin to wonder aloud whether we may have happened upon a decisive "moment of truth" for pastoral theology in our time.

THEOLOGICAL ROOTS OF
PASTORAL PRACTICE

Theological foundations must be laid carefully. How is psychotherapeutic empathy analogous to the Christian good news of God's love? Empathy is the process of placing oneself in the frame of reference of another, perceiving the world as the other perceives it, sharing his or her world imaginatively. Incarnation means that God assumes our frame of reference, entering into our human situation of finitude and estrangement, sharing our human condition even unto death.

When the troubled person finds himself or herself under the care of someone with accurate empathy, someone who seems able to enter another's perceptual framework, he or she experiences a profoundly liberating feeling of being known, being understood. Empathy is the precondition of all therapeutic effectiveness.

Christian worship celebrates the God who has chosen to enter our human frame of reference, to participate in our troubled condition, and to affirm human existence by sharing in its contingency, suffering, and death. Just as the counselor enters the frame of reference of a troubled person and, without being neurotic, significantly participates in that person's neurosis, so God, according to Christian witness, participates concretely in our human estrangement without himself being estranged.

When the Apostles' Creed confesses trust in the one who was born of the Virgin Mary, suffered under Pontius Piliate, was crucified, dead, and buried, it expresses a penetrating affirmation of God's determination to share fully in our human condition. This stands against the docetic view that Christ was never really born. The early church witnessed to the infinite scope of God's unconditional empathetic love. Analogously, the therapeutic process may be seen as a certain sort of descent into hell. The therapist engages in the depths of the inner conflict of the neighbor, descending into that hell with the other person. This may in turn free the neighbor to experience the hell of his or her own feelings, looking toward a renewal of faith and courage.

In all effective psychotherapy there is hidden an implicit assumption that is made explicit in the Christian proclamation. The therapist accepts the troubled neighbor in the midst of neurotic guilt feelings and compulsions, not on the narrow assumption that the neighbor is just privately acceptable by the therapist as a friendly human being, but on the much more basic assumption that every person, as human being, is accepted by being itself. Effective empathy assumes a cosmic permission to get in touch with one's own deepest experiencing. Persons who are offered this empathic gift tend to grow toward more appropriate self-acceptance and self-understanding. The counselor is not the source of such acceptance. The counselor only points to an acceptance that has its source beyond himself. The unspoken assumption is that acceptance is already there, despite all human rejection, and that the person who is neurotically guilty, anxious, and depressed does not have proper self-knowledge. The assumption that the individual is acceptable is a more profound ontological assumption than is ordinarily acknowledged by the therapist, who does not arrive at this assumption, but begins with it.

This implicit assumption is precisely what is made explicit and revealed by God's self-disclosure in Jesus Christ. The Christian proclamation seeks to state clearly and decisively that in Christ God has made himself known to us as one who loves us so unconditionally that his love calls for radical behavior change on our part. The Source of life is *for* us. This Word is declared not as a speculative idea but in and through an event. The ministry of Jesus of Nazareth is the originative event that calls forth the witness of the church to this Word from on high.

Can Christian proclamation of this unmerited divine grace be made consistent with humanistic-Socratic counseling which seeks the achievement of insight? A clearer conception of the self-disclosure of the accepting reality may help us hold together both sides of a seemingly paradoxical answer: The Christian good news is that God is with us and for us, which is the implicit basis of effective therapeutic empathy. That implicit awareness becomes explicitly announced in Christian preaching.

When the empathic pastor works effectively as a counselor, faith is becoming active in love. Here proclamation and therapy support one another in an integral ministry of witness and mission. The love of God to which the pastor overtly witnesses in preaching is recapitulated in a nonverbal way in the active empathy of counseling.

But why even preach, if the same accepting reality is fully present in so-called secular relationships? What is the point of talking about Jesus as the Christ if the love that he manifests openly is hiddenly present in all of life and perhaps uniquely and dramatically in secular psychotherapy?

This same basic issue is to be found already in the New Testament. Paul declares that "there is no distinction between Jew and Greek; the same Lord is Lord of all and bestows his riches upon all who call upon him" (Rom. 10:12, RSV). Yet if God is already present, why announce his presence? Paul explains that the purpose of proclamation is to call persons to an awareness of the reality of the situation in which they already exist, the reality of God's occurring love; not to introduce God to the world as if God were not already there, but to introduce persons to themselves as those who are always already claimed by God. Paul asks how are we to rely upon the accepting reality if we have never known ourselves to be encountered by it (Rom. 10:14)? And how are persons to "believe in him of whom they have never heard? And how are they to hear without a preacher?" In sum: "Faith comes from what is heard, and what is heard comes by the preaching of Christ" (Rom. 10:17, RSV). Here is the necessity of overt, clear, decisive proclamation, which announces the accepting reality present in therapy as a reality that has chosen to make itself bodily known once for all in history.

Suppose we pursue the other side of the issue. If proclamation of the revealed Word of God is necessary in order to identify the ground of acceptance, why should it not therefore become imperative that the therapist always be a preacher, an overt proclaimer of the self-disclosure of the accepting reality? The nub of this issue is whether divine acceptance must be mediated verbally or whether it can be adequately mediated nonverbally through an interpersonal relationship. Our argument hinges on the premise that liberating divine acceptance can be mediated concretely through concrete interpersonal relationships without overt witness to its ground and source, although it is also seeking constantly to clarify through language its inner source and ground.

THE POINT OF VIEW OF MY WORK AS AN AUTHOR

It was in an attempt to spell out the intriguing consequences of these embryonic insights and hunches of the late 1950s that I set my feet on the path that has preoccupied me ever since—the attempt to reengage the then atrophied dialogue between theology and the many approaches to psychotherapy.

A summary glance over the road I have thus far taken will show more clearly where I am coming from. I want to speak autobiographically of the circuitous course of my own dialogue with psychotherapy, its challenges and limitations, and of the ways I am now coming to see the incompleteness of my own pilgrimage. I hope you will recognize that the surprising place in which I now find myself in this dialogue is an organic extension of the basic concern that first drew me into it. Otherwise, my present classicist trajectory might, on superficial glance, seem to be an unexplained reversal of the previous direction.

My clinical beginning point in the 1950s, later surpassed, was client-centered therapy. I myself was a recipient of the accurate empathy and unconditional positive regard of an extraordinarily congruent person, Robert Elliott. So I speak of these relational qualities as one who experienced them as profoundly important at a particular juncture of my life, 1955–56. By the close of the fifties I was seeking as a young teacher to effect a workable integration of a therapy of personal self-disclosure with a theology of divine self-disclosure (more particularly of Carl Rogers and Karl Barth).[1]

In the mid-sixties I was in Germany doing clinical work at the Psychiatrische und Neurologishe Klinik of Heidelberg, enthusiastic especially about existential psychotherapy, asking whether the tradition of Martin Heidegger, Ludwig Binswanger, Karl Jaspers, Medard Boss, J. H. van den Berg, Igor Caruso, and Viktor von Weizsäcker could be integrated into the secularization theologies of Dietrich Bonhoeffer and Rudolf Bultmann, to which I was then deeply committed.[2]

In the "freaked-out" late sixties I was eagerly investing myself in almost every available brand of intensive group process from T-groups and growth groups to microlabs and marathons with a strong emphasis on psychodrama and Gestalt awareness training. I did more clinical work in the psychiatric ward of a VA hospital, and taught Clinical Pastoral Education chaplain trainees at the Institute of Religion of the Texas Medical Center. I looked for some connection between contemporary group process and the Jewish-Christian tradition of small group confession and mutual pastoral care, especially as manifested in Jewish hasidic and Christian pietistic groups of the 18th century.[3] But even at that point I began to recognize the potential self-deception of my own antinomian temptations. Like most liberal Protestants of that period, I had deep-seated tendencies to anarchic politics and messianic expectations about social experimentation, which (under the tutelage of my inimitable friend, Will Herberg) eventually revealed themselves as hollow. This work with experimental groups extended into a more chastened critical study of transactional analysis in relation to Pauline-Augustinian understandings of human bondage and freedom.[4]

About 1971, however, there was a major turn in my pilgrimage as I gradually became painfully aware of the so-called outcome studies reporting the dubious effectiveness of average psychotherapy, whose cure rates barely match spontaneous remission, coupled with the frightening spectre of client deterioration (i.e., patients finding their condition worsening under the care of professional psychotherapists). The sobering implications of these controlled studies for pastoral care elicited a substantial shift of direction for me toward the kind of critique of pychotherapeutic assumptions that was already being developed by Thomas Szasz, O. H. Mowrer, Hans Eysenck, and William Schofield.[5]

My work with experimental group psychotherapy and interpersonal analysis essentially came to an end in 1976. I had been attempting to solve some of the problems strewn in the path of transactional analysis. I thought the TA simplisms needed a basic corrective. So I developed the Collusion Spectrum as a more accurate descriptive means of sorting out human interactions, relying heavily on the empirical data of several social psychologists, mostly of a behaviorist orientation (George Homans, J. Thibaut, H. Kelley, the early Timothy Leary, Robert Carson, and Harold Rausch). I sought to correlate these data with the medieval doctrines of virtue and interpersonal justice.[6]

The crisis intervention therapists (Eric Lindemann, Gerald Caplan, Robert Carkhuff, David Switzer, and Edgar Jackson) then became important to me in the mid-seventies as I dealt with the more sober moral dilemmas involved in pastoral care for the dying.[7]

Although I had been teaching Kierkegaard seminars for many years and had lived in constant companionship with his authorship, the perennial Kierkegaardian side of my work did not bear visible fruit until I completed a work on Kierkegaard's parables, which was fully two decades in the making.[8] No twentieth century psychologist has influenced my psychology as deeply as Kierkegaard, and I still doubt that the analytical powers and psychological insights of Freud and the post-Freudians have equaled those of Kierkegaard.

This circuitous account of my pilgrimage is crucial to the rest of what I will be saying. For it forms the background of the work I am currently trying to do in the recovery of the classical pastoral traditions. By 1979 a very different theological project was undertaken—the attempt to recover classical ecumenical orthodoxy amid postmodern cultural consciousness. That effort represented a joyful decision on my part to turn again toward the classical Christian pastoral tradition, especially as expressed by the ecumenical consensus of Christianity's first millennium of experience in caring for souls. It was coupled with a critique of modernity, which I define as the overarching ideology of the modern period characterized by the three key terms describing larger patterns familiar to modern psychotherapy—autonomous individualism, naturalistic reductionism, and narcissistic hedonism. Modern chauvinism has assumed that all recent modes of knowing the truth are vastly superior to all older ways, a view that has recently presided over the precipitous deterioration of social structures and processes in the third quarter of the twentieth century. My frank goal has been to help free persons from feeling intimidated by modernity, which while it often seems awesome is rapidly losing its moral power, and to grasp the emerging vision of a postmodern classical Christianity.[9]

This is a rough aerial map of the rocky ground I have covered in trying thus far to relate therapeutic counseling to the Christian message. As I now return to the early Christian pastoral tradition, however, I do not wish to negate the learning of this earlier journey of psychological discovery, nor do I want to disown my own work except for a few brief excessive passages in which I harshly inveighed against a deliberately religious orientation in counseling. But I now see more clearly than before some of the deficits that prevented the previous dialogue from deepening and maturing. So this is where I am coming from—but where am I headed?

PART 1

THE DILEMMA
OF MODERN
PASTORAL CARE

CHAPTER 1

Recovering
Lost Identity

A major effort is needed today to rediscover and remine the classical models of Christian pastoral care and to make available once again the key texts of that classical tradition following about fifty years of neglect, the depths of which are arguably unprecedented in any previous Christian century. A whole generation of pastoral scholars will be needed to recover textually and rediscover practically the classics of pastoral care, texts which reach out for the contemporary working pastor in the counseling task. This book presents one such patristic voice, Gregory the Great, as a primary exemplar of classical pastoral care, but there are many others whose works need to find their way back to contemporary pastoral practice.

CLASSICAL PASTORAL CARE:
A TEXTUAL DEFINITION

Many of the key classical sources which have carried enormous weight for centuries of Christian pastoral counseling are available now only from rare book sources. Pastors and religious counselors today are hungering for deeper rootage in a tradition that is in many cases not even available to them.

The identification of the classical style of Christian pastoral care is best achieved by pointing to a series of venerable texts that have been repeatedly and resourcefully used as key reference points for the church's pastoral ministry, many of them steadily for over a millennium. These texts begin essentially with the New Testament Pastoral and Catholic Epistles and continue through many stages of development—patristic, medieval, and reformation—well into the nineteenth century, where pastoral theologians as varied as Horace Bushnell, Alexander Vinet, and Washington Gladden demonstrate that the tradition was diligently remembered and often quoted.

Although this is a richly varied body of literature, I will mention only a few of the most widely quoted sources that have often carried the essential burden of the tradition. Our purpose at this point is to show in a preliminary way that there is in fact a classical pastoral tradition and that this tradition is embodied in a well-defined series of texts: Cyprian's writings on patience, jealousy, and envy; Tertullian's works on the soul; Chrysostom on the priesthood; Ambrose on the responsibilities of the clergy; and numerous works by Augustine—on the soul, happiness, admonition, patience, and grief counseling.

At the center of the pastoral tradition is Gregory's *Pastoral Care*, which for more than a millennium was considered to be the indispensible guide to pastoral counseling; followed by Bonaventure on the right ordering of the soul; various sections of Thomas Aquinas' *Summa Theologica* on happiness, fear, anger, the emotions, the dispositions, love, and desire; Hugh of St. Victor on preparation for confession, anointing of the sick, and care for the dying.

The Reformation tradition of pastoral care is seen in Martin Luther's table-talk and letters; Zwingli on the pastor; John Calvin's letters; Martin Bucer on visitation of the sick and poor; Thomas More's prison writings; George Herbert's *Country Parson;* Gilbert Burnet's discourse on pastoral care; Jeremy Taylor's spiritual exercises; Richard Baxter on self-acquaintance; the astute English tradition of pastoral direction represented by Anglican Bishops Wilson, Spratt, Gibson, and Hort; many eighteenth century writers such as Philip Doddridge, Count Nicolas von Zinzendorf, Jonathan Edwards, John Wesley, and William Paley, who were all interested in pastoral care and the caring community.

They were followed by the pivotal contributions to the study of practical theology by F. D. Schleiermacher, J. M. Sailer, Claus Harms, Wilhem Loehe, H. A. Koestlin, J. B. Renninger, Theodosius Harnack, J. T. Beck, and Carl Immanuel Nitzsch in the nineteenth century German tradition. In the English tradition J. H. Newman, F. D. Maurice, Charles Bridges, and Handley Moule made key contributions, while the Swiss Protestant tradition was wisely represented by Alexandre Vinet.[1]

The preliminary list could be much longer, but at least this will serve to show where some of the basic textual materials lie for the restudy and redefinition of pastoral counseling today, lost as it appears now to be in what Erikson would call an "identity diffusion."[2] Although there are fascinating varieties within this tradition, a careful examination will show that it is indeed a single developing tradition rather than a plethora of unrelated traditions. It is unified by its eucharistic center and its concern to embody the living Christ through interpersonal meeting.

RECENT CLINICAL PASTORAL COUNSELING: HAS PASTORAL IDENTITY BEEN MISPLACED?

What curious fate has befallen the classical tradition of pastoral care in the last five decades? It has been steadily accommodated to a series of psychotherapies. It has fallen deeply into a pervasive amnesia toward its own classical pastoral past, into a vague absent-mindedness about the great figures of this distinguished tradition, and into what can only generously be called a growing ignorance of classical pastoral care.

In order to test out my hypothesis that the classical pastoral tradition has been quickly and abruptly forgotten in the twentieth century, I gathered some data from the indexes of leading books on pastoral theology from the nineteenth and twentieth centuries. I selected ten key figures in classical pastoral care that seemed to me to carry the tradition most significantly: Cyprian, Tertullian, Chrysostom, Augustine, Gregory the Great, Luther,

Calvin, George Herbert, Richard Baxter, and Jeremy Taylor. I then checked out the number of times they were referred to in seven standard works of pastoral theology in the nineteenth century, those by William G. T. Shedd of Union (Presbyterian),[3] Patrick Fairbairn of Glasgow (Scottish Presbyterian),[4] James M. Hoppin of Yale (Congregationalist),[5] Charles Bridges (Church of England),[6] Heinrich Koestlin of Giessen (Lutheran),[7] Washington Gladden of Columbus (Congregationalist),[8] and Daniel Kidder of Drew (Methodist).[9] I found that every one of these authors unfailingly quoted Chrysostom, Augustine, Luther, Calvin, Herbert, and Baxter (Table 1). There were 154 references in all to our

TABLE 1

**Representative Nineteenth-Century Pastoral Writers:
Frequency of References to the Classical Pastoral Tradition**

	SHEDD (1879) Presbyterian	FAIRBAIRN (1875) Scottish Presb.	HOPPIN (1884) Congregationalist	BRIDGES (1829) Church of England	KOESTLIN (1895) Lutheran	GLADDEN (1891) Congregationalist	KIDDER (1871) Methodist	TOTAL
CYPRIAN	–	1	1	6	2	–	1	11
TERTULLIAN	2	1	2	1	1	–	–	7
CHRYSOSTOM	1	2	6	13	6	3	2	33
AUGUSTINE	9	1	1	37	2	2	1	53
GREGORY	–	–	1	6	2	1	–	10
LUTHER	6	1	4	22	11	5	1	50
CALVIN	8	1	1	25	3	2	1	41
BAXTER	8	7	2	37	3	3	1	61
HERBERT	1	1	4	19	1	4	1	31
TAYLOR	2	1	3	7	2	2	–	17
Totals	37	16	25	173	33	22	8	314

ten classical pastoral guides. Most often referred to were Augustine, Luther, Baxter, and Chrysostom, followed by Herbert, Calvin, Taylor, and Gregory. This clearly establishes the point that at the turn of the century the classical tradition was alive and well, recalled, and considered important to the practice of pastoral care.

Curiosity aroused, I then selected seven major contemporary writers on pastoral counseling whose influence I judged to be most general and whose views seemed by consensus to be most representative. I chose the most widely used texts of four well-known Americans—Seward Hiltner, Howard Clinebell, Wayne Oates, and Carrol Wise,[10] and three Europeans—from the Lutheran tradition Dietrich Stollberg, from the Reformed tradi-

TABLE 2

Representative Twentieth-Century Pastoral Writers:
Frequency of Reference to Classical Texts of Pastoral Care

	HILTNER	CLINEBELL	OATES	WISE	TOURNIER	STOLLBERG	NUTTIN	TOTAL
CYPRIAN	0	0	0	0	0	0	0	0
TERTULLIAN	0	0	0	0	0	0	0	0
CHRYSOSTOM	0	0	0	0	0	0	0	0
AUGUSTINE	0	0	0	0	0	0	0	0
GREGORY	0	0	0	0	0	0	0	0
LUTHER	0	0	0	0	0	0	0	0
CALVIN	0	0	0	0	0	0	0	0
HERBERT	0	0	0	0	0	0	0	0
BAXTER	0	0	0	0	0	0	0	0
TAYLOR	0	0	0	0	0	0	0	0
Totals	0	0	0	0	0	0	0	0

tion Paul Tournier, and from the Roman Catholic tradition Father Joseph Nuttin of Louvain.[11] In all these major modern pastoral works I could not find even a single quotation by or reference to Augustine, Baxter, Calvin, Cyprian, Chrysostom, Gregory the Great, or Luther (Table 2). It is as if for these contemporary pastoral counselors classical pastoral thought did not impinge relevantly on their work.

This further whetted my interest in seeing how many references these same current writers might be making to key modern psychologists and psychotherapists in their attempt to give guidance to Christian pastoral counselors. I selected six major psychotherapeutic contributors—Freud, Jung, Rogers, Sullivan, Berne, and Fromm—and found 330 references to these modern figures in the same seven widely used texts, including 109 references to Freud, 101 to Rogers, 45 to Jung, 27 to Fromm, 26 to Berne, and 22 to Sullivan (Table 3). In most cases these writers were being quoted with approval or referred to as authoritative guides for pastoral counseling.

TABLE 3

Representative Twentieth-Century Pastoral Writers: Frequency of Reference to Modern Psychotherapists

	HILTNER	CLINEBELL	OATES	WISE	TOURNIER	STOLLBERG	NUTTIN	TOTAL
FREUD	8	8	9	1	9	5	69	109
JUNG	10	6	1	0	13	3	12	45
ROGERS	19	18	4	6	0	26	28	101
FROMM	8	6	0	9	0	1	3	27
SULLIVAN	5	4	5	5	0	1	2	22
BERNE	0	19	6	0	0	1	0	26
Totals	50	61	25	21	22	37	114	330

This exercise astonished me. It provided preliminary evidence for a hunch I had felt for a long time—namely, that contemporary psychotherapists are far more inwardly important and objectively authoritative for pastoral counseling today than are the writers of classical Christian pastoral care. I invite others to check this out for themselves, using different historical and contemporary writers; I think the result will be the same.

What happened after 1920? It was as if a slow pendulum gradually reversed its direction and began to swing headlong toward modern psychological accommodation. A key figure in the reversal was Anton Boisen, founder of the clinical pastoral education movement, a creative man in whom the classical tradition still lived and whose works are still eminently worth reading.[12] But after Boisen, pastoral care soon acquired a consuming interest in psychoanalysis, psychopathology, clinical methods of treatment, and in the whole string of therapeutic approaches that were to follow Freud.[13] It was a vital and significant task, but regrettably the theological moorings were not sufficiently deep to prevent an ever-increasing drift toward forgetfulness of the previous traditions of pastoral counseling. It is as if a giant shade had been pulled. Classic pastoral wisdom fell into a deep sleep for about four decades.

During these decades we have witnessed wave after wave of various hegemonies of emergent psychologies being accommodated, often cheaply, into pastoral care without much self-conscious identity formation from the tradition. I do not want to exaggerate so as to suggest that the classical tradition of pastoral care was entirely forgotten. That did not happen (as we can see especially in the brilliant work of Frank Lake).[14] We are still living implicitly out of the quiet influences of that vital but inconspicuous tradition. It is amazing how resilient these patterns of pastoral response can be, even when they are not being deliberately studied. For language assumptions and recurrent historical paradigms may continue to be maintained at operational levels by social traditioning, despite rapidly changing ideologies and leadership elites and the appearance of novelty. But the classical tradition has not been diligently studied since the 1920s. It has lain fallow and borne only occasional wild fruit. We are now at the far end of that pendulum swing, and the momentum is again reversing toward an emerging hunger for classical wisdom.

During the past twenty-five years of my professional life the methodological key to the active energies of pastoral care has been its pervasive hunger for the accommodation of various therapies from orthodox Freudian and Jungian all the way through the broad and colorful spectrum of Harry Stack Sullivan, Carl Rogers, B. F. Skinner, Erich Fromm, Fritz Perls, Eric Berne, Albert Ellis, Will Schutz, and Joseph Wolpe,—all of whom one by one have been courted and welcomed and accommodated (often rather uncritically) into the practice, structures, language, and professional apparatus of Christian ministry. The task of the pastoral counselor thus understood in recent years has tended to become that of trying to ferret out what is currently happening or likely to happen next in the sphere of emergent psychologies and adapting it as deftly as possible to the work of ministry. In the adaptation, however, the fundament of Christian pastoral care in its classical sense has at best been neglected and at worst polemicized. So pastoral theology has become in many cases little more than a thoughtless mimic of the most current psychological trends. Often these trends, as psychologist Paul Vitz has astutely shown, have been bad psychology to begin with.[15] Modern pastoral counseling has had only the slenderest accountability to the classical pastoral tradition. Meanwhile it is little wonder that the working pastor continues to look in vain to the field of pastoral theology for some distinction between Christian pastoral care and popular psychological faddism. I may be exaggerating slightly, but I think not much.

This process might plausibly have continued further for some time to come were it not for the most damaging and embarrassing blow to such accommodationism—the studies of psychotherapeutic effectiveness. I refer to the slowly growing recognition of the fate-laden importance of the so-called outcome studies disclosing the actual results attained through application of the various psychotherapies. Slowly but surely we are finally learning more and more about the surprising ineffectiveness of average psychotherapy. An accumulation of controlled studies by highly respected psychologists (Allen Bergin, Hans Eysenck, Hans Strupp, Jerome Frank, Charles Truax, Robert Carkhuff, and Philip Hanson) has convincingly shown that the average psychotherapy cure rate is about the same as that which eventuates merely through the passage of time, approximately 65-70 percent.

This is not just somebody's curious idea or untested theory, but a well-supported conclusion based on over three hundred controlled empirical studies.[16] These outcome studies have caused me to question the effectiveness of the very psychotherapies upon which I had earlier been building my case as a theologian in dialogue with behavior change theories. The evidence has been accumulating for a long time, but to date it has been almost systematically ignored by the accommodationist trend that has until recently become virtually normative in recent American pastoral care. The accommodation of pastoral care to psychotherapy has bottomed out proportionally as these empirical outcome studies have been taken seriously.

These data prompt us to return to the thornier question: Has bondage to the assumptions of modern consciousness resulted in the loss of our freedom to learn from the classical pastoral tradition? I think the short answer, at least in the U.S.A., is yes. The longer answer could be stated in the form of a hypothesis for further discussion: Recent pastoral counseling has incurred a fixated dependency upon and an indebtedness to modern psychology and modern consciousness generally that has prevented it from even looking at all premodern wisdoms, including classical pastoral care. This has amounted to a net loss of freedom, a harsh constriction on the freedom to learn. We have bet all our chips on the assumption that modern consciousness will lead us into vaster freedoms while our specific freedom to be attentive to our own Christian pastoral tradition has been plundered, polemicized, and despoiled.

Evidence is growing that the time is ripe for a major restudy of classical Christian pastoral counsel. The average pastor has come to a saturation point with fads. By now most have likely done the TA trip, the T-Group trip, microlabs, and perhaps some Gestalt training, as well as dabbled with psychoanalysis and/or any number of other available therapeutic strategies—client-centered, bioenergetics, Jungian, Adlerian, rational-emotive therapy, parent effectiveness training, EST, and the list goes on and on.[17] Pastors are anxiously wondering not only how most of these approaches are to be integrated into the Christian tradition (since many of them are openly contemptuous of key assumptions of Christianity) but also what their social and historical consequences will be. Early readings are not reassuring.[18] Wise pastors know there has to be a better way. They are often tired of compliantly following psychiatric clues in an era in which psychiatry itself is more and more on the defensive and at times in public disrepute. Many pastors have long suspected what the public opinion analysts are now verifying, that psychiatry has the lowest trust rating among all medical specializations.

It is doubly ironic that the psychologists and psychotherapists are themselves beginning to call pastors back to their traditional pastoral identity. Major statements by therapists Karl Menninger, Frank Lake, Paul Pruyser, Hobart Mowrer, Ruth Barnhouse, and Paul Vitz[19] have forcefully stated this point, and there is every reason to believe that the momentum in this direction will increase. In speaking of the religious counselors he has worked with, Paul Pruyser writes, "I became aware that much of the instruction was one-sided, with the consent of both parties: the theologians sat at the feet of the psychiatric Gamaliels and seemed to like it. Pastors were eager to absorb as much psychological knowledge and skill as they could, without even thinking of instructional reciprocity. . . . I have learned that ministers would be hard put to know what to teach, from their own discipline, to members of the psychological professions even if they were specifically asked and salaried to do so, "[20] and he goes on to plead that ministers recover their historic identity in order better to serve persons who are doing some real "soul searching."

A high priority for some theological teachers and pastoral care professionals will be to study, translate, and make available the texts that are now largely unavailable. Many of the most important of these valued treatises simply cannot be purchased. I know of nowhere that you can buy, even through rare book channels, Bishop Burnet's *A Discourse of the Pastoral Care* (1692), or Sailer's *Pastoral Theologie*,[21] you will find them in only a handful of the best libraries in the country. Some works like Augustine's "The Care to be Taken for the Dead" appear in the Nicene and post-Nicene Fathers, but the ailing translation is so jumbled as to be virtually unreadable. The translations of the Anti-Nicene Fathers and the Nicene and Post-Nicene Fathers, done prior to the turn of this century, are greatly hampered by stilted Victorian phrases. So we have several strata of problems: inaccessibility, out-of-print volumes, the high cost of rare books, poor translations, and add to this the hesitation of book publishers to risk publishing historical themes that are not self-evidently of wide popular interest. These are the obstacles that have stood in the way for some time now in bringing these texts back into availability. The hunger is rising as the nonavailability increases.

THE PROMISE OF AN ENRICHED SYNTHESIS BETWEEN OLD AND NEW

At this point it seems fitting to speak, even if tentatively, of the challenge and promise of the road ahead for Christian pastoral care, assuming a gradually increasing accessibility of the basic texts of the tradition. I am not proposing a reactionary archaism that would rigidly repeat culturally determined prejudices of the past. Nor am I proposing a radically new model that would transcend this morass with some brilliant innovation.

The task that lies ahead is the development of a postmodern, post-Freudian, neoclassical approach to Christian pastoral care that takes seriously the resources of modernity while also penetrating its illusions and, having found the best of modern psychotherapies still problematic, has turned again to the classical tradition for its bearings, yet without disowning what it has learned from modern clinical experience.

In order to do this we must learn in some fresh new ways the courage to give intelligent resistance to the narcissistic imperialism and hedonistic reductionism that prevail both in the culture and, to a large extent, in the churches. This course I have not yet seen, but nothing is more crucial for us in the pastoral care field than to find its ground and possibility. We can no longer afford ourselves the luxury of allowing contemporary psychotherapies to define for us what pastoral care is. The situation comes very close to being a confessional moment (*in statu confessionis*) for those of us to whom the teaching office of the church is committed, at least in the fields of pastoral theology and pastoral care. We must define for ourselves again what pastoral care is and in what sense pastoral theology is and remains theology, and in order to do that we must be carefully instructed by the tradition out of which that understanding can emerge. Otherwise there can be nothing but continued and expanded confusion about professional identity.

The task is not merely that of giving skeptical, critical resistance to present trends, but also that of giving new energies to a wholesome reconstruction of a pastoral care that is informed by Christian theology, able to provide a credible pastoral theodicy; able to work through difficult cases of conscience; aware of the dialectic of grace and freedom, gospel and law; able to point saliently to the providence of God in the midst of our human alienations; aware of the intrinsic connections between community, healing, and proclamation (koinonia, therapeia, and kerygma); and well-grounded in the classical understanding of the triune God. The prevailing theological method of recent pastoral care has followed the intuition of pietism in placing its stress largely on personal experience, often to the exclusion of historical experience, reason, scripture, and tradition. The new efforts in neoclassical pastoral care must work out of a sound, wholesome theological method that neglects neither scripture, tradition, reason, nor experience in the quest to understand how our response to revelation manifests itself in concrete personal and interpersonal decision.

But really, you ask, what can the classical tradition usefully contribute to modern pastoral counseling? What practical difference might it make if it were trying to preserve and develop the achievements of contemporary clinically oriented pastoral care? Although it is far too early to answer these questions with any certainty, there are some general shifts of direction that to a greater or lesser degree I would expect to occur:

• Intercessory prayer would again become an important aspect of pastoral counsel.

• The antinomianism of contemporary pastoral care (under the tutelege of hedonic pop psychologies) would be more effectively resisted by a more balanced dialectic of gospel and law.

• Marriage counseling would tend to function more within the framework of a traditional Christian doctrine of matrimony rather than essentially as a hedonic cost/benefit calculus.

• Empathy training for pastoral counseling would be more deliberately and self-consciously grounded in an incarnational understanding of God's participation in human alienation.

• Out of our recent history of exaggerated self-expression, compulsive feeling disclosure, and narcissism, we may be in for a new round of experimentation in askesis, self-discipline, self-denial, and rigorism, which might in turn threaten to become exaggerated in a masochistic direction and thus again need the corrective of a balanced Christian anthropology.

• The diminished moral power of the previously prevailing momentum of individualistic autonomy and self-assertiveness may call for a new emphasis in group process upon corporate responsibility, mutual accountability, moral self-examination, and social commitment, an emphasis that would be undergirded by studies in Bible and tradition.

• We are ready for a new look at the traditional Protestant pattern of regular pastoral visitation, which could enter many doors now closed to most secular therapists.

• Pastoral counsel would work harder than it is now working to develop a thorough and meaningful pastoral theodicy that takes fully into account the philosophical and moral objections to classical Christian arguments on the problem of evil and the meaning of suffering, yet with new attentiveness to the deeper pastoral intent of that tradition.

• The new synthesis would interweave evangelical witness more deliberately into the process of pastoral conversation rather than disavowing witness or disassociating proclamation from therapeutic dialogue.

• Group experimentation would continue, but be rooted with more awareness of classical Christian understandings of witness, service, and community.

• Older therapeutic approaches such as fasting, dietary control, meditation, and concrete acts of restitution would have new importance.

• The now atrophied concept of call to ministry may need to be thoroughly restudied and reconceived as a hinge concept of the pastoral office and of ordination.

• Contemporary pastoral theology in dialogue with the classical tradition may learn to speak in a more definite way about the spiritual and moral qualifications for ministry, reflecting the tradition's persistent concern for moral character, humility, zeal, and self-denial.

• The arts of spiritual direction that have been developed, nurtured, reexamined, and refined over a dozen centuries of pastoral experience may be due for serious restudy. Efforts could be made to bring these resources back into contemporary pastoral interactions that presuppose post-Freudian understandings.

• Pastoral care would become less prone to messianic faddism, because it would have built into it a critical apparatus more deeply rooted in the Christian tradition.

• A nonsexist, nonchauvinist reinterpretation of ministry, prayer, pastoral care, and spiritual direction would require a serious critical dialogue with tradition, a dialogue that must be as far-ranging as the radical feminists assert and yet able to incorporate the collective wisdom of Christian historical experience. Such critical dialogue is worth risking and far better than a simplistic accommodation to modern individualistic narcissism or reductive naturalisms.

• The term pastoral counseling would again be reclaimed as an integral part of the pastoral office, intrinsically correlated with liturgy, preaching, and the nurture of Christian community and relatively less identified with purely secularized, nonecclesial, theologically emasculated fee-basis counseling.

THE MOMENT OF TRUTH

Pastoral counseling need not be ashamed of many of its achievements in the twentieth century. But it cannot boast of its biblical grounding, historical awareness, or theological clarity. The European churches are learning rapidly from American pastoral care of our clinical training, supervisory programs, and therapeutic skills, but if we ask how well we have integrated these achievements into ordained ministry, or a clear conception of the pastoral office, the answer must be—"very superficially." At worst, pastoral counseling has learned that it can get along quite well without Christ and the apostles, scriptures, ancient ecumenical church teaching, and with minimal pastoral reference. At times it amounts to a curious disavowal of professional ministry in the name of professionalism.

I have tried as a theologian to defend fee-basis counseling. In the past I have even sought to provide for it a biblical and theological rationale. But today I find myself hard put to account for the now all-too-familiar pattern of the ordained, full-time, fee-basis pastoral counselor who has no congregation, no explicit pastoral role, and cannot tell you the inner relation between the therapeutic task and the Christian community. One has to skate pretty far out on the thin ice of secular theology in order easily to embrace the premise that this is all there is to the pastoral office—diakonia without marturia, counseling without kerygma—and that pastoral counseling may be fully expressed without any reference to Christian revelation, baptism, Lord's Supper, ministry, ordination, prayer, scripture, and the language of the religious community out of which the counseling emerges and to which it is presumably accountable.

Protestant and Catholic pastoral counseling has been drawn into a collusive relationship with an accommodationist theology that has seduced it into a partial or substantive disavowal of historic Christianity, its sacraments, doctrine, ordination, and self-giving service. I give you a case in point: with the emergence of government supported therapies, to our amazement it has now suddenly become a pocketbook question for some fee-basis counselors as to whether they are in any definable sense Christian pastors, and on that answer hangs the fateful possibility of their being able to get on government payrolls as counselors and consultants. The specter of government sponsored pastoral counseling not only raises grave questions of church and state boundaries: it also raises puzzling questions about the extent of disavowal of religious orientation and witness implicit in tax supported counseling.

This has thus unexpectedly placed pastoral counseling at a confessional crossroad (*in statu confessionis*).[22] Some will experience the question starkly: As a pastoral counselor, will I in good conscience accept income from the government at the cost of disavowing implicitly or explicitly all religious perspective or reference in my counseling process? If I make that disavowal, to what extent can I or the church I serve legitimately regard that as pastoral counseling? What is specifically pastoral about a pastoral counseling that has abandoned the historic pastoral office? Some "professional pastoral counselors" will answer, "Yes, I can in good conscience accept government funding," using as a precedent other ministers who have entered government social services. They will argue that they can fulfill their ministry without word and sacrament, without overt witness or worshiping community, and (why not?) without ordination. Big brother government involvement in pastoral counseling is only an overt and stark example of what is happening more subtly in fee-basis pastoral counseling generally, with third party payments on the increase.

What disturbs me most is the fact that such fateful decisions can come so easily and thoughtlessly. For I am aware of the cheap grace theology that supports them, which I myself to some extent have condoned or at least (until recently) not rejected with determination. That theology has offered pastoral counseling a fleshless Christ, a *logos asarkos,*[23] coupled with a diluted ideology of general ministry that makes no distinction between the ordained ministry and the ministry of the laity, and therefore easily loses track of the specific scriptural entrustment to ordained ministry to secure the apostolic witness through Christian teaching, preaching, and sacramental action.

Just as the Christian martyrs of the second and third centuries were called upon by state power to give assent to the Roman gods, and because they refused entered into a *status confessionis* in which confession of faith was unavoidably required at great cost, so ministry today is coming to such a point where this confession of faith is unavoidable: We will not accept your tax money, surveillance, or support if they require any hint of a disavowal of the God of Abraham, Isaac, and Jacob, and Jesus.

Some will choose one way, some another. But if it is less than a deliberate decision, we deceive ourselves in a deeper way than all the layers of neurotic self-deception that we have learned to analyze. For it is, finally, God with whom we are dealing, who judges justly, and who knows the imaginations of our hearts.

CHAPTER 2

Why Gregory?

We now introduce the pivotal figure who will occupy our attention throughout the remainder of these pages. In doing so, we will show why Gregory is a perennially plausible model for pastoral integration. We will seek to clarify the principal assumptions that shaped his distinctive approach to the guidance of souls.

GREGORY WHO?

Who was this character? Why should we return to writings that are now almost fourteen centuries old? Why is it appropriate that we look at his life, even if briefly? He taught that the surest witness to the authenticity of a teacher is his embodied behavior. It is hardly possible to speak properly of his theology apart from his unusual life.

Gregory is surely one of the most gifted persons in Western history. He had enormous influence on both the thought and the life of the medieval church, its organization, its mission, its forms of worship, its songs, preaching, and scriptural interpretation. He almost single-handedly developed a holistic pattern of theological and pastoral integration of the sort that we are still searching for today.

More than that of any theologian from Augustine to Luther, Gregory's pastoral work had awesome political effect—so much so that it has become axiomatic that to understand the Middle Ages, one must understand Gregory. Just as Augustine's theological formulations were essential to medieval Christian theology, so Gregory's pastoral formulations were essential to the formation of medieval pastoral life. It is not unusual for church historians to divide pre-Reformation church history into two essential parts—before Gregory and after Gregory. For Gregory fittingly sums up and concludes the patristic period. And the medieval period begins with his transitional work, based on a firm Augustinian footing. Gregory is considered one of the four great Latin Fathers (along with Ambrose, Jerome, and Augustine) and is usually viewed as the principle founder of the medieval papacy.[1]

Gregory is popularly remembered for one contribution above all else—music. He was a music teacher, a musician, a composer, founder of the most influential school of music of his day, and the prime figure in the development of finely crafted Gregorian music. What other form of music can one name that has survived intact for more than a millenium?

The historical situation into which he was born was chaotic and frightening. It looked as if the ancient world was at that time being dismantled piece by piece. New nations were emerging. Barbarian powers were challenging ancient civilities. Pastoral theology during this period became not only the bearer of the Christian tradition but also of ancient culture and philosophy. Gregory was intent upon defending the achievements of ancient culture from irrevocable destruction.[2]

Born in A.D. 540 of patrician parents who owned large estates in Sicily and Rome, Gregory lived through a demanding series of extraordinary cultural crises and trying personal challenges. Between the time he was six and twelve years old (546–52) Rome was captured by the Goths under Totila, later garrisoned by Belisarius, again beseiged by the Goths, and once again conquered by Narses. It may have been this chaotic historical context that later elicited a rugged historical realism bordering on historical pessimism in Gregory, who sincerely expected that the world historical tragedy would soon come to an end. The constant threat of anarchy may have given him a different attitude toward temporal power than he would have had if he had been born in less troubled times. His social location as a recipient of wealth makes all the more dramatic the fundamental decision in his early thirties to give away all his possessions to the poor and take up the monastic life.[3]

Any reader of Gregory quickly senses the man's dialectical astuteness. His power of analysis reminds one of Socrates, Augustine, Kierkegaard, or Reinhold Niebuhr. All of these minds were able to hold together irony, paradox, and humor in good-spirited dialectical tension. They grasped the saliently competitive sides of a perplexing issue, pursuing the truth dialogically. Their habit of balancing statements with counterstatements makes the reader aware that they had taken seriously the crucial objections to their own arguments. Such was Gregory's mind. He displayed the kind of wisdom that habitually reflects discretely about the consequences of what one is saying.

This dialectical bent of mind led Gregory early toward the study of law and the practice of political service. His rhetorical skill and gifts of leadership soon became widely recognized. As a very young man of thirty-three years, having already served in various political offices, Gregory was offered and accepted the highest civil office in the city of Rome—that of prefect. Yet he held this office only a short time. Having quickly reached the pinnacle of political power in one of the most important cities of the world, he just as readily gave up the life of political governance voluntarily for the monastic life of poverty and prayer.

When his father died, Gregory became the inheritor of vastly wealthy Sicilian and Roman estates. Then came the critical turning point of his life. After a profound inward struggle, he decided once for all to give these far-flung properties to the poor. He completely disavowed both wealth and power. In 574, at the age of thirty-four, taking the oath of poverty and celibacy, he became a monk according to the pattern of St. Benedict. Through his energy and beneficence six monasteries were established in Sicily and one remarkable monastic experiment in Rome, St. Andrew, from which so much of the seventh century leadership of the church was destined soon to come. He gave all else to the poor. Later, when Gregory would urge the whole church to give liberally to the poor, he was commending, not an abstract idea without any radical commitment of his own, but rather a maxim that he himself had decisively embraced at the crucial moment of his life.

The monasteries followed a rigorous daily order of work and worship, of praise, confession, and study. They withdrew from worldly affairs in order to intercede for the world before God in prayer. Gregory entered wholeheartedly into this proto-Benedictine way. Later he recalled these monastic years (574–78) as the happiest of his life. During this period he improved the arts of spiritual contemplation and, as mentor to fellow contemplatives, applied himself to learn the elements of pastoral counsel.

In 578 his life turned again toward a public direction. He was abruptly called out of the monastic life, which he loved, into public life, which he resisted. There is abundant evidence from his private letters that he preferred the monastery, but against his own inclination he was persuaded in 578 to respond to an important historical crisis. The Lombards had been attacking from the north, advancing toward Rome. The only hope of help was thought to be Constantinople. The pope, Pelagius II, chose Gregory as his nuncio, a crisis diplomat. Gregory consented to become the ambassador of Rome to the court of Byzantium, an awesome responsibility that he was to hold for six difficult years (579–86).

While in Byzantium, he learned that if Rome were to survive it had to do so on its own resources; it could not look always to Byzantium or Ravenna for help or protection. That information became a crucial lesson that would have much significance later when he was to acquire much wider responsibility.

One might imagine that the cosmopolitan city of Constantinople would be an inhospitable place for the quiet and thoughtful Gregory. With the help of several monks who moved to

Byzantium with him, however, he was able to maintain his monastic disciplines, holding together the balance between the contemplative and active life. He was both monk and ambassador without ceasing to be either. It was there in Constantinople that he completed his first major theological work, on the morals of Job, or *Moralia,* a discussion of moral maxims and insights that emerged out of his metaphorical exposition of the text of Job.[4]

The last noteworthy event of his stay in Constantinople was his debate with the Patriarch of Constantinople on the critical question of the resurrection. Gregory argued for the palpability of Christ's resurrected body, against the notion of an impalpable, unbodily, immaterial resurrection—a *logos asarkos.* This was for Gregory a hinge point of Christian teaching that could not be diminished without dire consequences. The conflict was finally adjudicated by the emperor in favor of Gregory.

Upon his return to Rome, Gregory soon became the key soul guide at St. Andrew monastery. Under his guidance the monks had wide effect upon distant parts of the known world. Vivid glimpses of monastic life of that time are seen in Gregory's *Dialogues.* Gregory's views of spiritual formation were decisively shaped through this intensive group experience. He lectured on the prophets, the historical books, and the wisdom literature of the Old Testament, to which his metaphorical imagination was irresistibly drawn.[5] But the community of prayer was the decisive context for this creativity.

Out of the abbey of St. Andrew came many missionaries to Spain, to the Lombards, to Sardinia, and—most importantly—to England. It was to this period that the story as told by the venerable Bede and the monk of Whitby belongs, of Gregory's memorable encounter with young Anglo-Saxons in the market (perhaps slaves), of whom he remarked: *"non Angli, sed angeli"* (not Angles, but angels). Gregory and his fellow monks began to conceive a mission to the English. He obtained permission from the pope to go to Britain and actually set forth on his mission. But when the people of Rome learned that he had left town headed for England, and was to be gone for a long time, they protested urgently to the pope. The local crowd of pursuers caught up with the departing band of missionaries on their third day out from Rome and, it is said, virtually forced Gregory to come back to Rome. Shortly thereafter Gregory took up the duties of papal secretary to the ailing pontiff.

It was from Gregory's closest circle of fellow monks, however, that the first missionaries to England shortly thereafter came, led by Augustine, Gregory's close friend from St. Andrew, who became the first bishop of Canterbury and the principle "Apostle to the English." Gregory's name is thus intimately connected with the origins of the Christian community in England. Later the early medieval king of England, Alfred the Great, presided over a translation of Gregory's *Liber regulae pastoralis* into Anglo-Saxon. This pastoral treatise became one of the earliest and best-preserved examples of primitive English style.

Even before Gregory's ascension to the papacy he had refined a remarkable combination of theological and pastoral interests: the dialectic between contemplation and action, the balance between orthodoxy and orthopraxis, scripture study practically applied, the combination of political activity with theology, and the concern for preserving the external safety of the Christian community amid an intermittently hostile political environment. Whether we approve of his political activities or not, there is no doubt that Gregory was politically concerned and imaginatively active in decisively impacting his own world. Yet at the same time he rigorously maintained the contemplative life. Although wealthy by birth, he was deeply committed to relieving and improving the lives of the poor. While ensconced in the heart of Roman Christianity, he envisioned a world-wide Christian mission and was himself willing to become a missionary to a remote and primitive people who showed vast promise. All these things were present in his ministry prior to the time that, upon accession to the papacy, he wrote his famous book of pastoral care, which will be the primary interest of the pages that follow.[6]

THE POPE AS PASTOR

The year 589 was a time of economic, military, and cultural disaster for Rome. Devastating floods followed by pestilence caused many deaths. The economy was moribund. Rome was constantly threatened with foreign invasion. Amid this dismal situation the aging Pope Pelagius II died in February of 590. Gregory, who had been serving as the pope's confidant and secretary since about 586, was immediately and unanimously elected. He knew, however, that the acceptance of the office meant the end of the contemplative life that he so much desired. So he resolutely refused to accept the office. It was more than a polite refusal. He went to extraordinary lengths to disavow the election. He addressed a letter to the Emperor Maurice pleading with him not to confirm the election. By some accounts he went for a time into hiding.

Six months later his election was finally confirmed by the emperor. Gregory was horrified at the news of his confirmation, having implored the emperor to be relieved. The clergy and people of Rome, who desperately wanted Gregory as pope, seized him bodily it is said, and carried him to the basilica of St. Peter. The unwilling monk was consecrated on September 3, 590. There is no doubt from subsequent letters that for the rest of his life he regretted his elevation. He truly wanted to remain a monk, a modest director of souls, and a quiet contemplative. Instead, the last fourteen years of his life were spent in an energetic and amazingly creative papacy. At last accepting the unwelcome challenge, he transmuted the office itself in irreversible ways.

His first act in the papal office was to write his remarkable *Pastoral Care*. A book of pastoral instruction, it was originally intended primarily for bishops, but its counsel also applied to all those serving as pastoral guides or in tasks of spiritual direction. It quickly became a standard handbook of pastoral care for subsequent generations. It was undoubtedly one of the most widely read works of medieval literature, so highly esteemed that centuries later in many episcopal areas bishops were formally presented a copy of the book during their ordination and pastors were instructed to follow its precepts. It became the prime interpreter of the tasks of pastoral care for over a millenium following Gregory. Of no other work on pastoral care can such a claim be made. The remainder of this book will be a critical analysis of its argument.

The plague ended soon after Gregory's succession to the papacy. Gregory was determined to find a way to peace with the attacking Lombards. Against heavy odds peace was finally concluded in stages between 592 and 593, but Gregory had to resort to making a separate peace when the civil authorities miserably failed. The price was high, requiring a costly ransom and continuing tribute in order to secure a stable peace.[7]

The pastoral care of the poor soon became the central preoccupation of his administration. He showed great skill in financial accountability and estate management. Those who had been managing the estates and papal patrimonies soon learned that they were not dealing with someone who could be easily deceived. They were required to be accountable. Gregory was exceedingly careful in watching over the temporal resources that were to be dedicated to the poor. He almost literally emptied the treasury of the papacy on behalf of the poor. He regarded himself as an administrator of this property for the sake of the poor, for whom one could never do enough. Due to wars, plagues, and floods, many refugees were strewn about the Roman countryside. No one who reads Gregory's letters can dismiss this man as insensitive to the dispossessed. He basically reconceived the purpose of the papal patrimony. These valuable lands in Italy, Sicily, Gaul, and Northern Africa had great resources which Gregory channeled toward care of the poor, the ransom of captives, and support of hospitals and orphanages.

One memorable clue to Gregory's servant image of the pastor emerged from a wrenching conflict that occurred between Gregory and John, Patriarch of Constantinople. In 595, John had assumed the auspicious title of Universal Bishop, which Gregory

thought to be self-serving and regrettable.[8] In order to demonstrate his own response Gregory publicly defined the role of the
Roman bishop as the servant of the servants of God (*servus ser-
vorum domini*), a term that thereafter was used to describe the
heart of papal authority and one which has been thereafter always
associated with the Gregorian political imagination.

Gregory's influence on liturgy and music matched his influence
on theology and ministry. He reformed the sacramentary of
Gelasius and set the mass very much in the shape in which it
remained until this century. Yet Gregory is remembered for
nothing more than his music. He is said to have instituted an
academy for cantors and given them lessons himself. Deeply fond
of music, he reformed the psalmody, wrote hymns and prayers
with musical accompaniment, and supervised the composition of
choral music for versicles and canticles. He saw to it that a stunning musical accompaniment would attend the Gregorian liturgi-
cal reforms.

Gregory did not think of himself as an original theologian. He
might have winced at the thought that he had changed or even
slightly revised any ecumenically accepted doctrine. Nonetheless
he was an imaginative orthodox thinker, in the sense that he
combined a commitment to orthodox church teaching (of the first
four General Ecumenical Councils) with a thoughtful and creative application of ecumenical orthodoxy.

His theology stressed penance as reparation. He thought that
some active behavioral response was required for the proper
reception of the Eucharist. Later this view became decisively
influential in medieval doctrines of penance and purgation. This
behavioral realism anticipates modern notions of behavior modification. For if you are serious about behavior change, Gregory
thought, you will work incrementally by small steps to modify
actually revisable behavior as evidence of your earnest desire for
change. One cannot truly repent and then sit around and do
nothing. Where that happens, repentance has been misun-
derstood.

Gregory is sometimes regarded as an original contributor to the idea of purgation of sins after death. But even this view correlated significantly with his view of contrition as requiring behavioral change and reparation. He was not proposing the unPauline view that one can merit God's forgiveness through good works. Rather through good works we show evidence of our seriousness about God's forgiveness. The omnipotent God visits the contrite through the grace of compunction, and the pastor declares the truly penitent absolved as a representative pastoral act. But this absolution does not abruptly end the task of soul care. For the penitent does well to show behavorial evidence of an earnest determination to live out the life of forgiveness. This is a distortable idea. It does not mean that our satisfaction supplants the satisfaction of God through Christ, but rather means that we work to amend the pain that our sin has caused by concrete acts of reparative penance. The truly penitent not only has a change of mind and a confession of the mouth, but also proceeds with some visible, demonstrative acts of restorative reparation, or deeds of penance. In Gregory we therefore have the kernel of the medieval doctrine of penance, the abuses of which Luther was later to recognize and struggle against. Otherwise Gregory's theology is strongly Augustinian, although less complex and philosophically sophisticated than Augustine's. Gregory's preaching became the pattern for much of the preaching and moral instruction in the early medieval period.[9]

Despite his wide reputation as a person of empathic kindness and understanding, Gregory's administration was known for its strictness. He was rigorous in oversight of church property on behalf of the poor. He was exceedingly discriminating in the appointment of new bishops, examining them carefully, not hesitating to reject one or propose another.[10] He was equally strict in taking away ecclesiastical privileges from clerics who abused their authority. He vigorously protected clerics from incursions or usurpations of authority by civil tribunals which had become unjustly extended.

Throughout his administration he had to deal with volatile

temporal authorities, notably with the Exarch Romanus of Ravenna, with King Agiluif of the Lombards and his family, and with the Byzantine emperors. He did not want Rome to be barbarized. He thirsted for peace, even on less than favorable terms. He was willing to look for available means of cooperation with the Emperor Maurice, and even with the Emperor Phocos after Phocos murdered Maurice. Gregory has been vilified by some Protestant writers for his willingness to work with whatever civil authority was in power. But this reflected his basic view of the relation of church and state. He viewed the emperor as God's representative for temporal authority and church leaders as guides of spiritual affairs. It was only when this preferred division of authority broke down that he was willing as pope to take emergency responsibility for temporal power. He struggled constantly for a benign cooperation between the two spheres. Each should take care of its own sphere without much interference from the other. He especially wanted ecclesiastical independence from state power and royal bungling. It was only when temporal power failed to protect innocent people that he resorted to raising an army, consulting with generals on military strategy, instructing ambassadors to the king, and negotiating a separate peace. Above all he viewed himself as called to intercede with state authorities on behalf of the poor and dispossessed when they were unjustly treated. He was not rebellious against temporal power because he thought it, according to Romans 13, instituted by God and accountable to God.[11]

Gregory protected Jews, championed their rights, and resisted the obnoxious practice of forcing them to accept baptism. He insisted on their civil freedoms and on respect for their right to worship in their synogogues. He also was willing to resist excessive or unjust practices on the part of Jews, especially that of owning Christian slaves.

Gregory was the first monk to become pope. He is for that reason sometimes called *pater monachorum*, the father of monasticism. But of course he did not father monasticism. Rather, he expressed its ideals and furthered its growth. He placed stringent claims upon monastics and granted them special privileges.

Even though he did not have the breadth of classical learning to match Clement or Origen or Augustine, he nonetheless was knowledgeable in the categories of Roman law, political thought, and medicine. He was the most important theologian of his century, in addition to being a brilliant administrator, a committed missioner, an imaginative biblical exegete, a beloved preacher, and above all a wise physician of souls.

This is the man to whom we appeal today as still relevant to our contemporary malaise in pastoral care. He is a man of many parts, with remarkably broad interests and versatile competencies. By all accounts he was remembered as a saintly soul and an inimitable soul guide.

KEY ASSUMPTIONS OF
GREGORY'S *PASTORAL CARE*

We are seeking to show how classical pastoral reflection offers a viable pattern for pastoral care today. From among many exponents of the classical tradition, we have chosen Gregory the Great on the grounds of his wide influence and his extraordinary pertinence to our contemporary dilemmas.

The whole range of Gregory's work reveals the scope of his pastoral-theological integration. The writing that most clearly and prominently displays the heart of this integration, however, is his *Liber regulae pastoralis* (literally Book of Pastoral Guidance), often translated as *Pastoral Care* after the first two words of the text (*Pastoralis curae*) or as *Pastoralia* or *Concerning Pastoral Care (De pastorali cura)*. To this, the most widely read single text in the history of pastoral care, may be added his letters of pastoral instruction to various persons in ministry concerning the special situations they were confronting. Of the many letters he wrote, 854 are extant. They cover widely diverse subject areas. Gregory also wrote biblical expositions on Job, a number of homilies on the Gospels, and twenty-two homilies on Ezekiel (593). Finally, he wrote four books of *Dialogue on the Life and Miracles of the Italian*

Fathers and the Immortality of the Saints (593–94), in which he re-counted the remarkable life of Benedict of Nursia, founder of the Benedictine order. This work became a model for early medieval hagiography.[12] We will focus mainly on one book, the *liber regulae pastoralis,* his systematic treatise on pastoral care, using his biblical exegesis and correspondence as supportive resources.

Only two English translations are available of Gregory's *Pastoral Care,* both regrettably dated. Henry Davis's 1950 translation for Vol. 11 of the Ancient Christian Writers Series (hereafter noted as *PC*) is better than the 1894 translation by James Barmby (here-after noted as *BPR*) for the Nicene and Post-Nicene Fathers (*NPNF*), though it, too, remains seriously deficient. Two limita-tions are particularly important: Davis rather woodenly translates *regula* consistently as *rule* rather than *pattern* or *model,* and he tends to render *monere* as *admonish* rather than *counsel* or *advise.* The impression is given that Gregory is addressing only bishops about matters of episcopal admonition and governance, instead of pastors generally about the whole pastoral task. Thus the pastor becomes a "supreme ruler" or "governor" who "rules" his flock, rather than a pastoral guide who provides wise counsel for the flock.

Among the recurrent themes of Gregory's pastoral book are these four axioms: (1) that each pastoral case requires variable response, (2) that the display of an outstanding virtue may con-ceal a corresponding vice to which the pastoral counselor must attend, (3) that the pastor's care mirrors Christ's care for us, and (4) that authority in ministry is paradoxically validated only through humble service following the example of Jesus Christ. We will briefly explore these axioms.

Gregory's most influential assumption is that no two pastoral cases are to be handled in precisely the same way. Each requires a response gauged to the specific contours of the situation. Gregory calls the pastor to be keenly attentive to these contextual peculiarities, fine nuances, and ever-changing emotive qualities, rather than flatly applying rigid norms without listening to the situation.

Second, an apparent virtue may often conceal a hidden vice or moral deficit. There was a cautious realism in Gregory's candid recognition that each desirable behavior or excellent action overtly displayed may betray or reveal a corresponding limitation or dysfunctional behavior. Gregory grasped clearly the inner complementarity of virtues and vices and was fascinated by their accompanying self-deceptions. Virtue was thought to be an appropriate balance of desirable behaviors. But Gregory was keenly aware that any excellent balance that is capable of being achieved is capable also of being easily upset in one direction or another, toward either an excess or a deficit, which is the essential definition of *vitium,* or *vice.* He understood how commonly vices pass themselves off as virtues, as when tightfistedness masquerades as frugality.[13] He illustrated: A parishioner who is wasteful may pretend to be generous. Likewise, "Often inordinate laxity is believed to be kindness, and unbridled anger passes as the virtue of spiritual zeal. Precipitancy is frequently taken as efficient promptitude, and dilatoriness as grave deliberation."[14] The analysis was rigorous and realistic.

Given these deceptions, it then becomes necessary for the discerning pastor to distinguish carefully between excellent behaviors that have intrinsic proportionality and those that are dysfunctionally excessive or deficient. At a broad level of generalization, Gregory's pastoral care sought to nurture in the parishioner an appropriate balance of excellent behaviors without the self-deception that invites vice to parade as virtue.

A central feature of the caring process involves sorting out the layers of self-deception that prevent one from seeing these imbalances. The pastor therefore becomes an agent of realism on behalf of the parishioner to clarify prevailing self-deceptions. This occurs through deeply empathic interior participation in the other's consciousness, deeply respecting the person. Through warmth, listening, patience, and spare advice, the pastor helps the parishioner to grasp and overcome the self-deception.

Third, our interpersonal care can at best be only a modest refraction of the radiance of God's own caring for us in Jesus

Christ. Throughout Gregory's *Pastoral Care* the christological analogies are constantly interplaying with and infusing the pastoral images. Christ is the true pastor whose caring is manifested through our care. Our comfort points beyond itself to the comfort of God in Christ.

There is in good pastoral care a sensitive and subtle balance between caring for the person's inward feeling process, and caring for the person's outward behavioral change.[15] God's care for humanity in Christ is aimed not just at the temporary luxury of immediately "feeling better about ourselves," but at the long-term reshaping of behavioral responses, taking practical steps toward implementing constructive changes in order that a more richly grounded happiness may become possible.

Finally, all who are given responsibility to guide others ought to "consider in themselves not the authority of their rank, but the quality of their condition, and to rejoice not to be over [persons], but to do them good."[16] The empathic pastor whose life is lived in Christ is able to see through historical distortions and class distinctions to grasp the fundamental unity and equality of persons. That respect for persons is reflected through the down-to-earthness of the good pastor, and it has its root in a christological analogy: God is empathic with us in Jesus Christ, therefore we are being called to be empathic toward the lonely or alienated neighbor. Whatever authority is given the pastoral office, it is paradoxically validated only when it is accompanied by the sign of humility, signaling that it shares in Christ's own empathy for human fallenness.[17]

GREGORY'S ANTICIPATIONS OF MODERN PSYCHOTHERAPY

One of the serendipities modern readers find in studying Gregory is that he seems to anticipate several psychological approaches and therapeutic developments that are currently considered to be wholly unprecedented innovations of contemporary psychotherapy. Imagined newness is often historical ignorance. Gregory anticipated modern therapies in five ways:

First, those who imagine that behavior modification techniques are a twentieth century innovation may have forgotten how prevalent some behaviorist assumptions have been in the Christian tradition generally, and particularly in the early medieval monastic and penitential traditions. Gregory's work emerged out of the creative milieu of the formative stages of Benedictine monasticism. He placed a strong emphasis upon the regular and consistent positive reinforcement of desired behaviors. He was intently concerned with the careful identification and accurate tracking of preferred behaviors, with deliberate scheduling of realistic behavior change objectives, with accurate measurement of incremental changes, with deliberately programmed steps of behavior change, and, at selected times, with aversive conditioning.[18]

Second, many think of Freud as an unparalleled innovator who first learned to unpack the hidden layers of unconscious motivation through an analysis of one's early interpersonal history, always alert to the tendency to self-deception and rationalization. Yet all these interests are recurrent dimensions of Gregory's pastoral method. Self-deception is assumed by Gregory to be a constant tendency of the fallen will. Reality based self-knowledge is one of the central aims of a healing process that proceeds by conversation. Some of Gregory's images—chiseling at the wall, opening the door, or going through the door and beholding the beastly, the animal, the libidinal images inside—are much akin to the kinds of unraveling of dream images and unconscious symbolism that we find later in Freud and the psychoanalytic tradition.[19]

Third, those who think of Jung as consummate innovator will find much in Gregory that anticipates Jung's affirmative view of the unconscious, of primordial fantasies, and his psychological fascination with mythic and mandalic meanings.[20] Gregory understood well the coincidence of opposites, and the imaginative resolution of opposites into a higher synthesis or integration. He was intrigued by the ways in which every vice is correlated with its virtue so that personal interaction becomes a constant interplay of these opposites, complements, and corollaries. Powerful archetypical images float in and out of Gregory's language and are constantly being treated imaginatively through his spiritualist biblical expositions.

Fourth, those who speak of the importance of body language and nonverbal communication may think of this as a distinctively modern notion,[21] but again they may be surprised to find Gregory constantly relating the caring process to nonverbal communication. Pastor and parishioner communicate not only through words but through acts, colors, symbols, clothing, and nonverbal gestures. Gregory was keenly attentive to the correspondence or lack of it between speech and life, language and act.

Finally, and perhaps most importantly, the three primary assumptions of client centered therapy were all operational already in Gregory's pastoral method. Carl Rogers identified these three necessary and sufficient conditions for positive psychological change as accurate empathy, unconditional positive regard, and self-congruence.[22] In subsequent sections we will show how each of these three points of the therapeutic triad function crucially in Gregory's pastoral care.

THE ART OF PASTORAL GOVERNANCE

Gregory's central subject is pastoral guidance (governance or direction) rather than the more limited notion of pastoral rule (as the available English translations would suggest). Although written chiefly for the pastoral guidance by and for bishops, Gregory's view of pastoral care finds many applications in all the pastoral offices, including deacons and presbyters as well. He teaches his readers how to become proper physicians of souls, able to recognize different spiritual diseases and to suit the treatment to the various cases so as to guide the soul toward spiritual health, toward happiness and wholeness, toward sanctification and fulfillment.[23]

The guidance of souls is an art exceeding all other arts in subtlety. It requires on the part of its practitioner accurate perception of complex data, a lifetime of scripture study, and practical wisdom. Objectively to understand spiritual precepts is not enough. A person may cognitively grasp and understand a precept yet not live in accordance with it. Pastoral counselors whose lives do not embody their teaching should not expect any prudent parishioner to take their counsel seriously.[24]

But how does one learn this art of arts, the governance of souls? "No one presumes to teach an art until he has first, with intent meditation, learnt it."[25] Some misconceive the difficulty of the counselor's task and prematurely yearn to "teach what they have not learned."[26] The problem is an old one, for Isaiah complained that "the shepherds themselves have not known understanding" (Isa. 56:11; cf. Jer. 2:8), and Jesus himself wryly observed that when the blind lead the blind, "both fall into the ditch" (Matt. 15:14).

We will show how Gregory weaves scriptural resources intrinsically into his pastoral care in such a way that biblical texts and pastoral practice are inseparable, and the one cannot be conceived without the other. Some modern readers may be vaguely disgruntled to find in Gregory only what their modern eyes perceive to be a naively unhistorical treatment of texts of scripture. If so, we are properly reminded that Gregory's treatment of scripture was exemplary of the typological, mystical, and anagogic hermeneutic that tended to prevail in his time. Neither Gregory nor any leading exegete of his time had a primary interest in objective historical evidentiary argument.

Gregory thought that a clearly conceived theory of pastoral care was required for effective pastoral practice. The art requires both study and personal mentoring.[27] The guide who proposes to take the flock through steep places, precipices, or hazardous situations must be fittingly prepared both conceptually and experientially. No one should enter this task of counsel of souls who has not practiced in life what has been learned by study.[28] Those who "penetrate with their understanding what they trample on in their lives"[29] are not yet ready for care of souls.

From Ezekiel, Gregory developed a powerful symbol of the potential danger that an egocentric minister may bring to the flock. It is as if the leading cattle trample the best herbage while they graze, or, when some come to drink, they churn up the water so others cannot drink. "My flock has to eat what you have trampled up and drink what you have churned up" (Ezek. 34:19). Gregory's analogy: A pastor may at first drink clear water, benefiting from the lofty wisdom of tradition, and graze in the pastures of scripture, but while he is in the pastoral charge he may be thoughtlessly churning up the clearest water and trampling the best grass from which others will later attempt to drink and feed.

Gregory thought that the pastor could create awful mischief for the congregation. "One who has the name and rank of sanctity, while he acts perversely" can do incalculable harm to the church.[30] Jesus rightly remarked it would be better that a millstone were hanging around one's neck than that one should harm defenseless "little ones" entrusted to one's care (Matt. 18:16).

Gregory thought the expectation of an easy income was the clearest evidence of the disqualification of the pastoral counselor.[31] Also, the hidden desire to "hold sway over others" was regarded as a particularly disastrous motive for ministry.[32] The overarching pastoral model is Jesus who refused coercive power when offered (John 6:15). When the "lust of preeminence" infects pastoral counsel, even good things that may have been achieved already may be undone and come to nothing in our hands. But when the pastor is willing to face adversity for truth's sake, then even evils of long standing can be wiped away.[33] Gregory illustrated the hunger for preeminence by reference to both Saul and David: Saul was a good man until he achieved power (1 Kgs. 10:22), while David loved God, but upon attaining power fell into infidelity and cruelty. The art of pastoral care is not won cheaply. When we try to snatch it as a means of manipulative power or personal control, it disappears in our hands.

THE HAZARDS OF SOUL CARE

Gregory was convinced that the guidance of souls carried special hazards for the guide. There is the danger that one may become so engaged in another's struggle that one decreases in

level-headed self-awareness. Ironically, in offering help the help-
ers may in time become more and more ignorant of themselves.
Preoccupation with the inner life of others may "dissipate the
concentration of the mind." It is as though one were "so preoccupied during a journey as to forget what [one's] destination
was."[34] When we are doing too many things for others without
realistically knowing ourselves, we may inadvertently harm
others. This is why rigorous preparation for pastoral counsel is
necessary: "We would not have [those] who stumble on plain
ground set their feet on a precipice."[35]

On the other hand those who have been called and prepared,
who are spiritually formed and theologically grounded, must not
refuse to undertake the risks of spiritual counsel. This would
deprive others of the gifts they rightfully should receive. The
maxim: One who fixates on one's own self-fulfillment so as to
ignore others' needs may not only deprive others of gifts prepared for them but ultimately deprive oneself of serenity. Jesus
said: "A city that is set on a hill cannot be hid" (Matt. 5:15). If you
love me, he said to Peter, "feed my sheep" (John 21:17). For those
who shrink from the task, who love only quiet and secret places,
Gregory's judgment is rather harsh: They are "undoubtedly
guilty in proportion to the greatness of the gifts whereby they
might have been publicly useful."[36]

In achieving a balance between self-care and care of others,
Gregory spins this homely analogy: With only one shoe, one
cannot walk easily. If one shoe is care of oneself and the other is
care for others, both are needed. He hinges this analogy upon an
amusing passage in Deut. 25:5–10, on which he happily dwells.
According to Mosiac law, in the case of a brother's death it would
be the surviving brother's duty to have intercourse with the wife
in order to continue the line of Israel.

> If the man is unwilling to take his brother's wife, she shall go to the
> elders at the town gate and say "My husband's brother refuses to
> perpetuate his brother's name in Israel; he will not do his duty by
> me." At this the elders of the town shall summon him and reason

with him. If he still stands his ground and says, "I will not take her," his brother's widow shall go up to him in the presence of the elders; she shall pull his sandal off his foot and spit in his face and declare: "Thus we requite the man who will not build up his brother's family." His family shall be known in Israel as the House of the Unsandalled Man. (Deut. 25:7-10).

Gregory's point (he savored these analogies!): If you are for others without caring for yourself, you have only one sandal. If you only take care of yourself, you have one sandal. If you are called and prepared to care for others and refuse, the circumstance is something like the woman who comes and takes the sandal off your foot and spits in your face![37]

Everyone who has seriously thought about ministry has encountered the special temptation that says, yes, I feel called to ministry but I do not want to be thrust into this gravely responsible position of guidance of souls. I would prefer, in the interest of humility, not to undertake any direction of souls. Gregory answered candidly out of his own intense struggle with his vocation: It is hardly genuine humility to refuse responsibility when you have understood that it is God's call for you to take a certain kind of leadership. Here the vice of obstinacy may be parading under the guise of humility. This vice gains its power from the burdensome awareness that we still do not desire to take on responsibilities for which we have in fact been thoroughly prepared because they run counter to our egocentric inclinations.[38]

CALL TO THE MINISTRY OF CARE

Gregory thought it hazardous to undertake the tasks of pastoral counsel without thinking deeply about one's pastoral calling. He used Isaiah and Jeremiah as laudable, but opposite, prototypes. Isaiah is the ready one who said, "Here am I; send me" (Isa. 6:8). Jeremiah oppositely pleaded with the Lord not to send him: "I do not know how to speak; I am only a child" (Jer. 1:6). Both are valid responses. Jeremiah repeatedly had to be prompted to accept the call to prophetic ministry, the same call to which Isaiah seemed to be eagerly drawn. It is good that Jeremiah, who had refused, did not persist in his refusal and that Isaiah, who wanted to be sent, was willing to become thoroughly prepared to be sent. Thus one who is called and prepared for care of souls must not egocentrically decline to undertake the task, or in the guise of humility proudly resist it. And yet one who is hesitant about speaking has the right to give due resistance to ministry until such time as the calling becomes clear and unavoidable.[39]

Gregory sees in Moses a proper combination of these two points of tension, which are brought together and integrated in the notion of humble consent. For Moses gave free consent to the task of leadership, yet he was fully aware of his own inadequacies. So we are called to resist, as Jeremiah did, the task of soul care in so far as we know our lack of preparation for it. Yet insofar as the calling is ascertained and preparation rightly made, we must, like Isaiah, consent willingly to the task.[40]

The same dialectic is found in the instruction to Timothy that "to aspire to leadership is an honourable ambition," which is immediately coupled with a rigorous list of desired behaviors that pastoral leadership should evidence, such as sobriety, good temper, courteousness, hospitality, and aptness to teach. The pastor "impels by approval and checks by alarms"[41] in a dialectic that requires multiple interpersonal competencies, both empathy and confrontation, reinforcing desirable behaviors and resisting undesirable behaviors.

Gregory was fascinated with the psychology of self-deception in the call to ministry: "For the mind often lies to itself about itself, and makes believe that it loves the good work, when actually it does not, and that it does not wish for mundane glory, when, in fact, it does."[42] We may deceive ourselves into thinking that once we have acquired the position of pastoral guide we will therefore respond magnanimously; yet once it is acquired we may quickly forget the compassionate energy that once motivated us. The remedy is sustained self-examination under the care of another experienced pastoral guide.

Effective ministry requires situational discernment, a due sense of which initiative is needed at which time. This is what the tradition has called "wisdom." For example, pastors may be "quickly moved by a compassionate heart to forgive," yet must not be so diverted by forgiveness that they forgive in excess or in such a way as to invite irresponsibility.[43] Only deep and accurate empathy can prepare the way for this discernment.

Gregory concluded Book One of his *Pastoral Care* with a remarkable exegesis of a curious passage found in Leviticus 21:

> The Lord spoke to Moses and said, speak to Aaron in these words: No man among your descendants for all time who has any physical defect shall come and present the food of his God. No man with a defect shall come, whether a blind man, a lame man, a man stunted or overgrown, a man deformed in foot or hand, or with misshapen brows or a film over his eye or a discharge from it, a man who has a scab or eruption or has a testical ruptured. No descendant of Aaron the priest who has any defect in his body shall approach to present the food-offerings of the Lord."[44]

Gregory does not take this passage literally, but he is fascinated with its symbolic meaning for those who provide counsel. Physical blemish is not his interest, but rather moral or spiritual deformation. Amusingly, Gregory focuses on the nose, metaphorically viewed: if it is too small, the counselor may not discern the stenches of human existence, but if too large, even as big as a "tower of Lebanon overlooking Damascus" (Cant. 7:4, RSV), such a nose will confuse itself by the variety of its own intake! Then the eyes are metaphorically treated: the bleary-eyed are not ready for offering counsel because their eyelids are weak and swollen by the flow, so they are not capable of fine, carefully balanced discrimination. Then the skin: one whose internal heat or undissipated anger is such that it continually breaks out in scabs and eruptions should not be charged with the care of souls, nor should one who has chronic skin itch, metaphorically a symbol of avarice. Finally, one who has a testical ruptured should not take on the task of spiritual direction, for symbolically that suggests an interpersonal style that easily becomes overburdened with guilt.[45] Whoever has these defects should not offer the loaves of bread. For one who is himself immobilized by these debilitating obstacles is not in a good position to reshape the immobilities of others.

PASTORAL CONVERSATION

One best prepares for pastoral counsel by meditating often on scripture and the patristic writers. It is only when one "pours continually on the examples of the fathers that went before him" and walks steadily in "the footsteps of the saints"[46] that the requisite wisdom and discernment will emerge. The pastoral guide is to "think without intermission on the lives of the ancients" (namely, the apostles, martyrs, and church fathers). It is only out of the life of dialogue with the ancient ecumenical tradition that the life of the pastor will be empowered and guided.

The pastoral guide points the way to others more by example than by overt instruction: "His voice penetrates the hearts of his hearers the more readily if his way of life commends what he says. What he enjoins in words, he will help to execute by example."[47] The soul guide must neither covet prosperity nor fear adversity. "Let neither smooth things coax him to the surrender of his will, nor rough things press him down to despair."[48]

Few learnings are more important to the pastor than to learn when to keep silent and when to speak. Two equal dangers must be avoided: either speaking what should be left unspoken or failing to speak what must be spoken.[49] The pastor must at times be like a bell—an open, clear, ringing public witness. But bells are irritating if rung incessantly. Bells are best heard sparingly and at the uniquely fitting time, especially at special, celebrative times (Exod. 28:33–35). The spiritual guide must not waste speech loquaciously but must save speech for the opportune moment of its greatest effect, when, symbolically, one may be able to "ring the bells" of another's moral awareness or self-understanding.

Gregory employed a sexual analogy for the pastor who is "addicted to much speaking."[50] Excessive loquacity is a little like lechery, like one who spreads his seed promiscuously. Good speech is more like a garden that is carefully weeded or a plant well-pruned. One produces a progeny of excellent thoughts with spare, well-ordered speech. But by spreading oneself out "in immoderate wordiness, he has an issue of seed, not for the purpose of progeny," but for self-assertive egocentricity. The pastoral counselor is duly warned against "uttering even that which is right overmuch."[51] Spare pastoral speech is compared to the pomegranate which has many seeds, all of which are ordered within a firmly formed outer rind—symbolic to Gregory of the unity of ecumenical faith (Exod. 28:34).[52]

AUTHORITY AND SERVANTHOOD
IN THE PASTORAL OFFICE

Order is the premise of freedom. Those who need assistance look to those capable of giving assistance. In the real world, parents and children do not stand on an equal footing, nor do teacher and learner. Yet soul care presupposes a more fundamental equality of human condition between the carer and those cared for.[53]

Gregory's essential metaphor for the pastor is, not the powerful king, but the lowly and patient shepherd. The influence of the shepherd is noncoercive and benign. Gregory recognized clearly a dilemma intrinsic to all pastoral leadership: guidance is necessary yet tends toward pride. Anyone who undertakes the office of ministry is tempted to look down upon others he is called to serve. Those who exercise influence or power perennially tend to deceive themselves into imagining that the accidents of power are based on merit. Gregory thought that this temptation accompanies virtually all forms of power or influence. We tend to assume that we are wiser merely because we temporarily have power. In exercising the influence of guidance, we easily forget our basic equality with others (Isa. 14:13).[54]

How is this dilemma of power to be ordered within ministry? Gregory wisely held this dialectic together: "He orders this power well who knows both how to maintain it and to combat it."[55]

Gregory's models for simultaneously maintaining and resisting pastoral power are Peter, Paul, and Jesus himself.

Peter, for example, deliberately refused to accept immoderate veneration. When Cornelius "bowed to the ground in deep reverence," Peter abruptly raised him to his feet and said, "Stand up, I am a man like anyone else" (Acts 10:26). Yet later, in the case of Ananias, Peter was fully capable of exercising bold, demonstrative leadership. Peter therefore was capable of both enjoying "the communion of equality" with those in his spiritual charge and asserting "the just claims of authority."[56] Only a proper grasp of this dialectical tension could have made Peter a credible pastoral guide.

Similarly Paul was a called apostle, legitimately recognized by the community as a teacher of faith, yet he approached the Corinthians with exceptional empathic affinity: "Do not think we are dictating the terms of your faith; your hold on your faith is secure enough. We are working with you for your own happiness" (2 Cor. 1:23). This dialectic fascinated Gregory because it showed so forcefully that Paul regarded the Corinthians as equal to him in faith and that his authority was not to be exercised except in abuses of faith. These three Pauline themes are closely interwoven—authority of apostolicity, equality of faith, and servant ministry. Paul had legitimate authority in maintaining the apostolic faith, especially where correction was needed. But he regarded himself as inconspicuously equal among believers.[57]

The pastor hopes to sustain this subtle, sensitive dialectic between authority and equality. The assertion of equality can tend toward excess if the ownership of legitimate governance is avoided. On the other hand, authority may be excessively exercised so that we lose track of our basic finitude and the equality of believers. Wisdom lies in a sense of due proportionality and accurate situational discernment. The pastor is called to exercise the legitimate authority of ministry, but to do so in a self-critical spirit so that parishioners may behold the Christ-centered connection between authority and servanthood.[58] Jesus distinguished between the Gentiles who "lord it over others" and you who are called "to serve" (Matt. 20:25). There is always a danger in ministry that under the pretense of exercising discipline we turn the ministry of governance into "the purpose of domination."[59] Yet on the other side there is another danger that in the interest of preserving the equality of persons we may fail to exercise needed discipline.

This equilibrium is illumined by a medical analogy: If you have a fractured leg, it needs to be compressed; by proper constraint, you hold back the fracture so as to prevent the wound from bleeding mortally for lack of firm binding. However, fractures can be made worse by immoderate constraint. To heal a wound, the bonds of constraint must be in the right proportion—not too tight, not too loose. Similarly, in ministries of care "there is much wanting to discipline and to compassion if one be without the other. . . . What one needs is both compassion justly considerate and discipline affectionately severe."[60]

Similarly, wine and oil, according to the medical practice of Gregory's day, were applied to wounds. Wine was used to cleanse and purify the wound as a purgative; oil was applied as a balm "to the end that through wine what is festering may be purged, and through oil what is curable may be soothed."[61] Similarly, pastoral gentleness must be mingled with firmness, and discipline with compassion. Only this combination of qualities makes a fit counselor.

The same dialectic is further symbolized by the rod and staff spoken of in Psalm 23. The rod is capable of restraint, while the staff provides support. Both are needed by the shepherd. Each is required in due proportion. Love must not be overpossessive, vigor must not be exasperating, and zeal must not be immoderately fiery. Rather, the pastor aims for a proportional blend of these caring qualities in all empathic counsel.[62]

Gregory warns against excessively wearying ourselves as pastors through overt action and praxis to the neglect of inner discipline and spiritual formation. One cannot provide good counsel for temporal happiness unless one has discovered that happiness which lives out of eternity. Gregory was critical of mindless pastoral activism that "delights in being hustled by wordly tumults" and yet remains "ignorant of the things that are within."[63] Timothy was similarly instructed: "A soldier on active service will not let himself be involved in civilian affairs; he must be wholly at his commanding officer's disposal" (2 Tim. 2:4). The pastoral counselor will not be inordinately involved in business matters or competitive enterprise.

Having stressed the importance of spiritual discipline, Gregory then turns to the importance of caring for one's own temporal and physical life. The pastor has a duty to his body; physical needs are not to be despised. Spiritual discipline that is careless of the body may quickly become dissipated.

It was said that the religious leaders in Israel would neither shave their heads nor allow their hair to grow too long. Rather, they were to clip their hair in a modest way so that it would cover the head but not fall over the eyes. Symbolically that suggested to Gregory that the pastor is not to be entirely cut off from the life of the flesh (as symbolized by the shaven head of the monastic), nor should hair grow so nativistically over one's eyes that one is unable to behold the light of eternity. The pastor lives between two worlds, eternity and time, body and spirit, in but not of the world.

TOUGH LOVE

The pastor must not be an advocate merely of what pleases the parishioner but more so of what ought to please.[64] The pastor, like others, is tempted to please others, to seek inordinately to be approved and loved, and to prefer flattery to the plain truth. To covet being loved is an understandable, and recurring, temptation in ministry.

The pastoral guide may be perennially tempted either toward softness or roughness in excess. If one is prone always to offer pillows and cushions for everyone (Ezek. 13:18), the dimensions of admonition and correction may be lacking, rooted in a "lust of trying to please." On the other hand the pastoral counselor may tend toward harsh censoriousness or excessive roughness, trying to coerce change in others, forgetting kindness, and resorting to tactics of fear in order to force behavioral change on demand. For a more appropriate balance of softness and roughness, Gregory turned to the biblical models of Peter, who willingly accepted Paul's rebuke (Gal. 2:11), and of David, who listened profitably to the straightforward reproof to Nathan (2 Sam. 12:7). Both counsels were uttered in the context of covenant love.

It is not surprising that the pastor has a desire to please others in a proportional way. But when this becomes linked with an excessive hunger for affirmation, one may lose candor and misplace truth. The pastoral desire to please needs a deeper purpose, namely, to draw persons nearer the truth. Pastoral conversation does not proceed merely to wallow in affirmation, but rather to live in the service of the truth. In this sense, the pastor does well to study to please others in order that a trust relation may be deepened. This is different from seeking affirmation for its own sake. Again Gregory's pattern was Paul, who sought earnestly to please all persons in all things (1 Cor. 10:33), yet maintained his capacity for candid negation and constructive reproof. "Paul pleases and does not please, because in wishing to please he sought not to please men, but that through him truth might please men."[65]

Gregory's pastoral care had room for the seasonable toleration of a persistently undesirable behavior. This medical analogy was used: If you apply medications that are unseasonable, not suited to the time or stage of the illness, they may entirely lose their medicinal function. The remedy must fit the precise time when it can be metabolized. If it cannot be currently assimilated, then the pastor may in good conscience deliberately tolerate the error and look for a better time for truthful disclosure.[66] The pastor, however, should be aware both of the potential collusive quality of such counsel and of its temporary necessity.

DEPTH COUNSELING

There are other times, however, when such temporary collusions are inappropriate, when some painfully deep unpacking
may need to be done. Note how similar Gregory's procedure is, in
this case, to that of modern psychoanalysis. When a matter is
deeply hidden in self-deception, it needs delicate examination.
Counselors may begin by examining little things, throwaway
comments, minor irritations. They will chip away at tiny deceptions, things so small they are almost unnoticable. Only then can
they find a window into the larger passions and motivations.[67]
First, says Gregory, the pastoral conversation makes a tiny hole
that later becomes a small door, which later may become a larger
door through which both conversants can walk through to see
what is inside.

To develop this procedure, Gregory commented upon a powerful metaphor from Ezekiel, who spoke of first digging at a wall
until there appeared a door, through which he then went in
where he beheld the "abominations," the hoary characters, the
fantasies of deceit. This, says Gregory, is what pastoral counselors
do. They first chip away by delicate probing, putting a wedge into
the situation so that the hardness of heart will in some sense be
softened or dented. Only then may there appear a larger door
through which one can move into the interior world of affect of
the neighbor. One may then go in and see what is there. In
Ezekiel's case, he beheld there "the creeping things" and the
"idols" (Ezek. 8:7–13, RSV). Gregory was suggesting a conversational procedure that resembles in some ways what we know today
as psychoanalytic therapy, where one "goes in, as it were, to see
the abominations," and by examining certain external symptoms,
"sees into the hearts of his subject, so that all the evil thoughts
therein are disclosed to him."[68] Here the counselor beholds the
beasts, the appetites, the idols, the creeping things. This is a
procedure for incrementally unpacking layers of self-deception,
moving from a dent to a door and then into the inner heart and
motivational roots of consciousness.

When should gentleness be the hallmark of counsel? Especially when the fault occurs as a result of ignorance. When finitude has played a greater role in freedom's fall, then "it is certainly necessary that the very censure of it be tempered with great moderation."[69] Pastors know that all flesh, including their own, is tempted toward infirmity, misconception, and corruption.

Here Gregory makes an astonishing observation akin to the psychoanalytic notion of projection: Whenever we are overly zealous in pursuing the infirmities of others, we may be fearing in them precisely what we are reproaching in ourselves. This is why Paul instructs the admonisher to "look to yourself, each one of you; you may be tempted too" (Gal. 6:1–2). Gregory elaborates: "It is as though he meant to say in so many words that when the sight of another's infirmity is displeasing, reflect on what you are, that the spirit may moderate itself in its zeal of reproving, in fearing in its own case that which it reproves."[70]

Some deficits are to be openly confronted and firmly encountered. This is especially so when the fault has been stubbornly left unrecognized. Then it must be called candidly to the attention of the hearer if any headway at all is to be made. Ezekiel suggests that there are times when you must virtually "draw a picture of it" (cf. Ezek. 4:1ff.).

Yet if this is done too harshly, such a recognition may drive a guilt-prone parishioner to despair. Immoderately sharp pastoral admonition may cut too deeply. It is said in Mosaic Law that if you go into the woods to cut wood with a friend in simplicity of heart and accidentally the axe flies from your hand, your friend may be hit and killed (Deut. 19:4–5). When an axe flies accidentally from the hands of an overzealous counselor, regardless of high motives, the wound may be too deep.

We have reviewed Gregory's views of the authority of ministry and the rudiments of pastoral counsel. The path is now clear to examine an extended series of cases of pastoral counsel that require discernment, good judgment, and contextual wisdom. Gregory has laid the groundwork by discussing the balance of virtues required of the spiritual guide, the dialectic of gentleness and severity, the recognition of vice that may parade as virtue, the relation of contemplation and action, and the need for silence as well as speaking. All of these themes are crucial in the preparation of the pastor for contextual discernment in pastoral conversation. Now Gregory turns to seventy-two case studies in pastoral response. These cases are the central concern of the remainder of his *Pastoral Care* and of Part Two of our analysis.

PART 2

CONTEXTUAL
PASTORAL COUNSEL

CHAPTER 3

Case Studies
in
Pastoral Theology

More explicitly than anyone else in the early pastoral tradition, Gregory the Great developed the theory and practice of contextual pastoral counseling. Its oft-repeated rudiments are found in the longest and most important section of his *Pastoral Care,* Book Three.

CONTEXTUAL COUNSELING

Having discussed readiness for ministry in Books One and Two, Gregory now turns to the interpersonal dynamics of pastoral conversation. His central question: How is the pastor to counsel or admonish (the Greek is *nouthesia,* the Latin, *admonitio*) those in his charge? Gregory's main premise: What is helpful to one may be hurtful to another.

In developing this thesis, he plays with these analogies: "Herbs which nourish some animals are fatal to others . . . the medicine which abates one disease aggravates another."[1] This is the overarching "principle of variability" that Gregory of Nazianzus had earlier grasped[2] but which now was systematically developed for the first time by Gregory. It was destined to impact powerfully upon many subsequent interpreters of pastoral care.

A single unified core of doctrine was assumed by Gregory. He presupposed an accepted orthodoxy, a standard conception of correct ecumenical teaching of the faith once for all delivered to the saints. Gregory insisted, however, that this unified teaching must always be accompanied by a variable practice of ministry that is constantly responsive to the changing personal needs and the here and now situation of the parishioner.

PASTORAL RESPONSE IN
PARADOXICAL CASES

Gregory developed an intriguing series of paradoxical case studies of the diversities of pastoral counsel. He showed how dissimilar problems must be dealt with in subtly differentiated ways. To illustrate: The combative person cannot be approached in the same way as the meek character-type. The self-assertive spirit requires a form of pastoral treatment different from that needed by the self-effacing. Those who give resources liberally are to be counseled in a distinctly different way from those prone to covet or steal. The shy are treated differently than the loquacious.

The pastor works constantly within these polarities. The impatient person is treated differently than the person who is patient to a fault. Some so fear reprimand that they live their lives in comically compulsive correctness. They must be dealt with differently than those who have grown so hardened in aggressiveness that they can hardly even be penetrated by anyone's reprimand. Similarly, the physically ill must be counseled in a different way than the healthy, males than females, poor than rich, employers than employees, and the overjoyed will receive different counsel than the depressed.[3]

Gregory's case materials grow in complexity as he proceeds with his analysis of pastoral variables. Those who are fully conscious of their misdeeds and yet continue to do them must be pastorally dealt with differently than those who have discontinued doing misdeeds and yet remain largely unaware of their having changed. One who cannot take the first step in a change process must be dealt with pastorally in a different way than those who frequently start to make changes but never carry them through to completion. Some do good publicly and evil secretly; they must be counseled in a wholly different way than those who may be prone to conceal the good they do publicly yet allow others to think badly of them publicly. This is the principle of variability, based on empathic listening to the specific situation of the parishioner.

All of these cases have one thing in common: God's eternal corrective love must be communicated to each one amid widely varied personal circumstances. Gregory systematically examines the differences in specific care for persons in these variable circumstances. Each case is one side, or vector, of a sharply defined situational counseling wisdom. What follows is an exploration of a selection of several of these thirty-six polarities of pastoral response.[4]

The Timid and the Assertive

The pastor may deal at one moment with a painfully timid soul and then be met in the next moment by one who is boorishly assertive. The pastor needs to have enough skill in interpersonal analysis to be able to recognize the difference in these ploys. Each requires a distinct pastoral response.

Gregory clearly anticipated some forms of transactional analysis that were to develop fully only in the twentieth century. For example, in an earlier study of interpersonal collusion in *TAG: The Transactional Awareness Game,*[5] I described the way in which both assertiveness and timidity function within a particular grooving of interpersonal relationships which I called the "assertive channel," in which one person has developed the excellent behavior of modest, sensitive self-criticism yet tends thereby to move excessively in the direction of self-effacement whereas the other person in the collusion may have developed the excellent behavior of self-starting independence but with temptations to arrogance. Gregory had an extraordinarily clear intuitive awareness of such dynamics in his analysis of the pastoral care of the timid and the assertive.[6]

According to Gregory, overly assertive persons are not likely even to recognize the degree to which they are being pushy or boorish. It may require a determined counselor even to awaken them to the recognition that they are overplaying their hand. Conversely, the timid are likely to be already painfully aware of their own inadequacies, especially of the tendency to impinge on another's territory or right. What is needed pastorally, according to Gregory, is not just supportive encouragement but also something like what we today would call assertiveness training. Gregory states this dipolar dialectic with exceptional accuracy: If assertive individualists need to recognize their tendencies to over-assertiveness, humble self-deniers need the opposite: to better grasp their low power position in order that they may offer to others more forthrightly what they are able to offer.[7]

Paul is viewed by Gregory as the pastoral prototype of one who could perform both types of contextual admonition in a well-integrated way. He could confront the aggressive individualist and increase the self-initiative of the overly timid without injuring the spiritual formation of either. He was quite capable of openly reprimanding the "foolish Galatians" who had become "bewitched" (Gal. 3:1, RSV), yet he responded quite empathically and supportively to the Philippians when they were already so painfully aware of their own inadequacies (Phil. 4:10ff.). The haughty and disdainful obviously require a different sort of pastoral sensitivity from those who oppositely may be unduly despondent about their own inadequacies. This is because the former think of themselves as lacking little or nothing, while the latter think of themselves as endlessly unprepared and structurally lacking.[8]

Suppose you are dealing pastorally with one of the latter type, a person who is already trapped in down-dragging syndromes of self-abasement, faintheartedness, and failure of nerve. Here the pastor's twofold procedure must be to "first praise that wherein he sees them to be strong, and afterwards, with cautious admonition, strengthen what was weak."[9] Gregory's biblical prototype for this is Paul's counsel to Thessalonians who were inordinately anxious about the end time: "I beg you, do not suddenly lose your heads or alarm yourselves, whether at some oracular utterance, or pronouncement" (2 Thess. 2:2). Thus, Paul's admonition for the timid was carefully linked with an assessment of their particular need for positive reinforcement and emotive support.

The Patient and the Impatient

Impatience is a special temptation of the powerful, who are forever inclined to underestimate the limits of their power. Submissive spinelessness is the peculiar vice of the accommodative parishioner whose virtue may tend toward an excessive patience that leads to immobility. In the pastoral office we often meet these two opposite types of parishioners. One will want instant compliance, while the other will be ready to comply immediately, looking frantically to others for guidance. These two persons, said Gregory, are to be counseled very differently.

Gregory offered a penetrating portraiture of the impatient person: agitated, not moving smoothly with time, always "ahead of time." Impetuosity often drives one toward precipitate actions. Many harmful secondary consequences come out of such impatience. When a consequent misdeed does occur, the impetuous individuals hurriedly fail to recognize its connection with their own impatience. This may cause them to undo what protracted labor had earlier accomplished, yet they hardly even recognize that it is their own impatience that has undone it.[10]

Such people need the kind of sensitive, straightforward pastoral care that can tactfully disclose to them precisely the moment when their impatience or agitation has precipitated undesirable secondary consequences for themselves and others. The key to the impatient character structure is that it tends inordinately to demand that everyone else comply quickly. Tempted always toward arrogance, the impatient are forever advertising themselves. They are often trying to manage an impression either of outward power or inward goodness. But they have not yet learned how to curb their self-assertive energies on behalf of others. Such persons are happy for good to be attributed to them, even if falsely.[11]

What kind of pastoral counsel is indicated? The scripture, with the help of the Spirit, says Gregory, can counsel best, that one had "better govern one's temper than capture a city" (Prov. 16:32). For to conquer a city is an external achievement, but to conquer oneself is a greater victory because it occurs within the sphere of freedom rather than through outward coercion. "In your patience possess ye your souls" (Luke 21:19, KJV), remarked Jesus. Gregory dwelt pensively upon the pastoral relevance of this text: Reason must possess the soul in patience if the soul is properly to guide the active life. We dispossess ourselves of ourselves when we lack patience because we disavow the rational influencing or shaping of the soul so that the body has no choice but to follow after an impatient soul, and thereby "we lose the possession of what we are."[12] We can lose ourselves out of impatience. The good counselor tries contextually to teach this to the impatient person.

Impatience draws us into a turbulent pace. Like the fool, we utter anything and everything on our mind (Prov. 29:11). We say things too quickly, without interior discipline, missing what the wise know, namely, that time is going to take care of much that elicits anxiety. The wiser individual learns to defer gratification and temporarily to curb libidinal energies in order to gain greater happiness.[13] This is why the wise are less exposed to the continuing hazards to which the impatient tend to be forever exposing themselves.

A very different type of pastoral counsel is needed for the person who may be patient to a fault. Patience is indeed a virtue, but all virtues are capable of being corrupted into vice. Patient people have their own hidden dilemmas. Having been patient under outward circumstances, they may be tempted inordinately to grieve over what they have suffered or missed. The limitation with which they have outwardly dealt patiently may have inwardly embittered them by the slow growth of suppressed indignation and resentment. They may become silently inflamed with bitterness.

Suppose the pastor is encountering just such a parishioner

whose outward life has borne patiently with severe limitations, having often adjusted and accommodated to others' necessities. Suppose the pastor's attentive listening, however, picks up underneath this extraordinary accommodation a tone of grief over some unspecified loss. Such a parishioner needs to face that grief. In time, and precisely through a conversational process, says Gregory, such an individual may come to hear through scripture the Spirit's address that love is not only patient but, as Paul immediately adds, also kind (1 Cor. 13). The superpatient individual may become inwardly festered with an interior malice which Gregory can only call "the mother of vices," because it is so much the opposite of that agape which is the root of all behavioral excellences. This is why Paul pastorally instructed the Ephesians, not just toward patience as if that were the only virtue, but also to work and talk and pray in order to be able to put away bitterness, indignation, and malice (Eph. 4:12).

Gregory set forth a psychologically complex and subtle analysis of the way in which demonic temptation functions in the consciousness of the excessively patient person. The temptations of fallen freedom are working simultaneously on two different fronts: first, to inflame insult and, second, to repay insult with insult.[14] The inordinately patient person has already conquered the first enemy, having borne with limitation. Yet temptation is not yet over, for it continues to work within the consciousness of the patient person by harassment, by secret suggestion, by laying hidden snares, by constantly reminding one of one's loss and of the insults one has suffered. These in time may tend to become grossly exaggerated so that they come to symbolize the way in which all of life has become insufferably insulting. In this way the mind of the overly patient person becomes vexed and disturbed.

Here Gregory develops two ironic analogies. The superpatient person is like one who has a very serious illness, who has come through the most dangerous phase of the illness yet later unexpectedly dies from a sudden relapse of fever; the fever was finally the cause of death.[15] Again, the superpatient person is like a soldier who has had a great victory in the field—the main battle is over; going into the city thinking the victory already secured, the negligent soldier is stupidly captured by a small, insignificant force within the gates.

The winner of patience has in a sense won the greater external victory and yet lost the struggle with quietly festering resentment. The spiritual gifts received through patience can be spoiled by malice. This inward battle of the patient individual is "visible under the divine scrutiny, and will become the worse, in proportion as they claim a show of virtue in the sight of men."[16]

FIGHTERS AND LOVERS

It is instructive to see how deeply Gregory intuited much of the interpersonal analysis that was later to be developed in the modern behaviorist tradition of vector analysis by G. Homans, R. Carson, T. Leary, J. Thibaut, and H. Kelley.[17] According to this modern behaviorist analysis, human interaction patterns can be graphed on the vectors of two poles: a horizontal emotive axis that registers resistance versus affection, and a vertical pole that registers superordination and subordination, or relative power or influence in relationships. In every interaction two parties relate to each other in terms of some positive or negative affect and some perceived upper and lower status, or relative power or acquiescence. Thus the two basic axes of interaction analysis are the resistance/warmth pole and the power/acquiescence pole.[18] Gregory had an uncanny intuitive sense of how interactions work along these two axes, even though the empirical research on them came fourteen centuries later.

Gregory recognized the need for different types of pastoral counsel for persons who come from opposite quarters of this spectrum of interpersonal preferences. Discordant and hostile persons are to be treated in a different way than pacific and intimacy-seeking persons. Those who are prone always to give aggressive resistance come from a different interaction posture than those who are prone to friendly ploys and encounters. In Gregory's terms the quarrelsome and the sowers of discord must be pastorally counseled in a different way than the affectionate and peaceful.[19]

What sort of pastoral care is indicated for the quarrelsome? They need above all to be addressed inwardly by the word of scripture that the fruit of the Spirit is love, joy, and peace (Gal. 5:22). This can be spoken credibly only by one who does indeed keep the unity of the Spirit in the bond of peace (Eph. 4:3). It is hoped that the perpetually discordant parishioner could be moved by gentle pastoral interaction to better grasp the disastrous social consequences of contentiousness. The reason unconstrained aggression is so potentially destructive to human relationships is that often it does not permit those subsequent goods to emerge which otherwise could have taken root if they had not been withered by the heat of aggression. Excessive discord breaks off relationships so that other interpersonal values cannot even be attempted. This is why Jesus insisted that if you come to the altar and remember that your brother has something against you, leave your gift on the altar and first be reconciled to your brother. Seriousness about interpersonal reconciliation is a precondition of seriousness about reconcilation with God.[20]

One may have acquired many other excellent interpersonal habits, yet lose their good effect because of this one disastrous tendency toward vituperative anger. You may have admirable courage, fidelity, discipline, and hope, but if you are prone to vindictive quarrelsomeness, the potential goods of those hard-won virtues may tend to become lost because of the antagonisms that have been unnecessarily elicited. The person of high intelligence is not thereby exempt from this temptation. Those who acquire power in the form of knowledge may find that it "separates them from the society of others, and the greater the knowledge, the less wise they are in the virtue of concord."[21]

Some are not just occasionally quarrelsome, but seem constantly, almost compulsively, to be looking for fights. Either deliberately or unawarely they create discord. The pastoral task is to help them grasp how potentially demonic and dysfunctional this habit formation may become. Gregory was convinced that "the enemy," a transpersonal demonic influence, was involved in this syndrome. Prov. 6:12 describes the behavior pattern of one who sows discord, who devised evil, who has a perverse mouth. Its spiritual root is an alienated will that has not learned how properly to order human loves. In this way charity, the mother of virtues, is extinguished. "Since nothing is more esteemed by God than the virtue of charity, nothing is more desired by the Devil than its extinction."[22] Pastoral counsel must then become a deliberate training ground in the possibility and value of sustained covenant relationships.

On the other hand, the pastor is destined to deal often with persons who are inordinately drawn to excessively quiescent, pacified, nonconflictive relations. Such persons will be prone always to sympathize with others, so as not to recognize the need for corrective candor or critical feedback. They are compulsively tempted toward tranquility. They are inordinately prone to flee to temporary peacefulness while failing to love well enough the peace of God which can challenge and disturb human tranquilities. The eternal shalom of God may interrupt and upset our outward forms of peace.[23]

This is why peace must be both loved and condemned. It is to be condemned insofar as worldly stability is immoderately loved. The parishioner who inordinately loves peace needs a pastor who will show a better way to meet conflict. The capacity for candor, confrontation, and encounter may be grossly truncated in one who has an inordinate fear and avoidance of human conflicts.[24] It is fitting to learn to provide resistance and critical negation to that which stands in enmity to the peace of God (Ps. 138:21). This is the ironic sense in which Jesus "did not come to bring peace, but a sword" (Matt. 10:34). There is in Jesus' message a healthy capacity for conflict and resistance. It is not simply naive love or costless reconciliation. The person who inordinately loves love, who in an excessive way desires to live in absolute peace, will need a mode of pastoral care that will foster growth in critical judgment.

The proper balance is again struck by Paul, who wrote: "So far as it is within your power, live peaceably with everyone" (Rom. 12:18, NIV). But this is a guarded statement with a qualifying clause: "so far as it is possible." This balance is what the counseling pastor must learn to grasp situationally, so as to recognize the difference between the need of the parishioner who is overly aggressive and the need of the parishioner who is trapped in a compulsive search for tranquility.[25]

The Powerful and the Acquiescent

In every interaction with another person there is some dimension of power, status, superordination or subordination, influence or acquiescence that enters into the relationship (unless the relation can somehow be maintained in a continuing equilibrium as precisely equal). In any given social organization there are differences of function in which some persons ordinarily exercise greater power and influence than others, while others are relatively more recipients of influence. The pastor deals with both the persons of power and the persons without power, persons with influence and persons without influence. Gregory argued that the pastor must learn how to deal resourcefully with both types without being either intimidated or insensitive.[26]

Persons who are relatively powerful, who are in charge of processes, organizations, or structures of influence may need pastoral counsel that will guide them away from the egocentric abuse of power and toward a more morally accountable use of power. Those who are relatively powerless or less influential may need to be counseled in a different way, so as not to allow themselves to be run over or demoralized. They need to learn the art of possibility, discovering what is possible precisely within the constraints of their time and place, and to do whatever can be done creatively within an intractably limited context.[27]

Gregory focuses on the relationship of parents to children. This is the arena in which scripture deals most prototypically with the right relation of power and powerlessness. The key New

Testament injunction has two interrelated parts: Children are called to obey parents; parents are called not to "exasperate your children" (Col. 3:20–21). The relation of parents and children stands as a broad paradigm of the possibilities and temptations accompanying all relationships of relative power and relative dependency. Scripture calls children to submit to legitimate guidance, but it is hoped that the guidance will be so wisely conceived as not to provoke children to anger.[28]

By analogy, if a parishioner is given power, or charged with leading an organization, or stands in a position of relative influence, then the greater is the weight and dimension of moral accountability. The employer for example, who fails even to try to correct manifest abuses eventually "comes to that state which his negligence deserves,[29] eventually becoming unable even to recognize the foibles and misjudgments of business associates. If you fail to give corrective admonition motivated by love, then not only will those in your charge remain uncorrected—you will therefore have failed in your duty to them—but things may drift into a worse state and you will fail even to grasp what has gone awry. When a leader disavows leadership, the whole body politic suffers.

Those with less influence need to be counseled in a different way. Precisely because they are in a privileged position of being less responsible for others, they are called to be more responsible for themselves!

What if power is abused? Gregory relates an amusing biblical story that illustrates a better way to challenge the abuses of power. Saul, who had unjustly treated David and was now pursuing him in the wilderness of En-gedi, had gone into a cave for the purpose of relieving himself. Hidden in this cave were David and his soldiers. The soldiers thought that David should attack Saul in his moment of inconvenience. David answered that one ought not to lay hands on the Lord's anointed, the legitimate ruler to whom obedience is due, the one who is called to preserve order. So while Saul was relieving himself David silently, stealthily crept up and symbolically cut off a noticable piece out of the king's cloak (1 Sam. 24:4ff.). Far from being an act of rebellion or an open attempt outwardly to overthrow abused power, it was a quiet, constrained, symbolic act that ironically caught the person of highest power in the midst of a most ordinary human activity. All this occurred harmlessly and unobserved, without Saul even knowing it. Saul's power was not overtly challenged in violent ambush, but its moral credibility was pointedly challenged and revealed as limited and vulnerable. For Saul later realized that David could have killed him then and there in the cave. David's restraint of power was grounded in his awareness of God's incomparable power. David and his soldiers could easily have seized power, but he chose a better way.

Gregory thought that this was an exemplary statement of the way to protest the abuse of coercive authority—not by overt, destructive, risk-laden rebellion, but by a symbolic demonstrative act revealing the vulnerable moral credibility of abused power. Yet even in this case, Gregory noted that shortly thereafter David was himself struck with grief merely because he had cut the hem of the king's robe. Even that, thought Gregory, was exemplary because it showed the sensitivity of David—the low influence partner—to the importance of maintaining order in society, that very order which had been abused but nonetheless remained necessary and tolerable even in its abuse.[30] The parishioner who has relatively less influence may need similar counsel: Do not prematurely seek to grab more influence, as if that were the only solution. Rather, acquiesce to legitimate authority. Exercise patience and tolerance. Continue to pray with serenity, even in the midst of the abuse of power. God is the Lord of both—those who have relatively more power and those who have relatively less (Eph. 6:9).

The Rich and the Poor

The pastor deals with all kinds of people, some of whom have relatively more economic power and prestige of ownership, some relatively less. Some people have extraordinarily great resources, while others are destitute of resources and even of the capacity to earn them. Pastoral responses to these varied cases cannot be the same. Those who have greater resources are to be counseled against pride and arrogance, while those with limited resources may pastorally need more the "solace of encouragement against tribulation".[31]

Gregory's ministry showed great concern not only for the practical, temporal, bodily care of the poor, as we have previously indicated, but also for the moral development of the poor. His central point: the poor deserve to hear the word of scripture, and the pastor has a duty to deliver that word to them. It is first of all a word of consolation. The poor are not to fear: "Fear not, you shall not be put to shame" (Isa. 54:4). But this counsel is linked with an eschatological promise that their descendants shall "people the desolate cities."[32] Out of a well-conceived pastoral theodicy, the pastor will help the oppressed to understand that their affliction may be a meaningful test of faith: "See how I tested you, not as silver is tested, but in the furnace of affliction; there I purified you" (Isa. 48:10).

On the other hand, the letter to Timothy suggested a different pattern of pastoral care of the rich:

> Instruct those who are rich in this world's goods not to be proud, and not to fix their hopes on so uncertain a thing as money, but upon God, who endows us richly with all things to enjoy. Tell them to do good and to grow rich in noble actions, to be ready to give away and to share, and so acquire treasure which will form a good foundation for the future. Thus they will grasp the life which is life indeed (1 Tim. 6:17–19).

The text does not say that we are to beg the rich, but rather that we are to instruct and charge them on apostolic authority that they not be "puffed up." They need this pastoral admonition if they are to understand that they cannot retain their wealth forever, and that they did not create the conditions for wealth. Otherwise the words of Jesus apply: "Woe to you that are rich, for you have received your consolation (Luke 6:24, RSV). The rich have completely missed the consolation of God if they simply consider this world their final consolation.[33]

Gregory's approach to pastoral care of the rich has exceptional subtlety, hinging importantly upon the biblical paradigms of Nathan before David and of David's care for Saul.[34] When pastors come before the wealthy as spiritual guides, they do well to remember what Nathan did in the case of the poor man whom the rich man had abused. The poor man had nothing of his own except one little ewe lamb that he had reared himself. It had eaten from his dish and drunk from his cup; it had nestled in his arms and was like a daughter to him. When a traveler came by and a local rich man wanted to display his conspicuous consumption but was too stingy to take something from his own store, he seized the ewe from the poor man and offered it to the traveler. That was the case study that Nathan presented to David, asking David what should be done. David answered angrily that the rich man deserved to die, and the poor man should be paid four times over for the stolen lamb. Nathan then said, "You are the man." Only then was Nathan in a sound position to confront David with his own sin in the case of his adultery with Bathsheba and the death of Uriah (2 Sam. 12:1–14).

Gregory found in Nathan's example a powerful model of how to proceed in a teaching ministry of pastoral care to the rich, who may be blind to their own pride and power and unaware of their own collusion with economic misery. The pastor proceeds by analogy so that the person being challenged will come up with a self-judgment based on the person's own conscience. The next crucial step is to help the person see clearly that judgment of conscience. Enabling one's conscience to become transparent to oneself constitutes a more significant pastoral service than harangue or castigation.

Gregory's corollary biblical paradigm comes from the complex relation between Saul and David. It is said that at times the only thing that would console Saul's depression was young David playing his harp. Whenever a "frenzied spirit" seized Saul, "David would take his harp and play on it, so that Saul found relief; he recovered and the evil spirit left him alone" (1 Sam. 16:23). Saul therefore made David his armor-bearer, and kept David with him constantly. From this interpersonal example, Gregory draws a broad analogy to illuminate the paradoxical relation of poverty and riches. There is a greater spiritual hazard in being wealthy and powerful than in being poor and powerless. The caretaker owes a duty to the rich to challenge them to use their resources responsibly, so as not to trust in the uncertainty of riches. Yet this may need to be done in the form of a harp, to soothe the madness of unchecked power gently by sweet tones. For riches intensify pride. Wealth gets itself locked into illusions that tend to block any form of corrective reproof. Therefore the harp must be used tenderly to stroke away the madness. But that is done only in order to come later to the point of a clearer pastoral attempt to nurture attitudes of mercy and justice as opposed to pride and inordinate trust in riches.[35]

The Intimidated and the Arrogant

Those who think of assertiveness training as an incomparably modern and recent innovation do well to examine some of Gregory's admonitions to the excessively humble. Some persons become so addicted to low status positions that they drift into winless dependency relationships. Others become oppositely addicted to excessive independence and haughtiness. These two polar types require different sorts of pastoral response.[36]

The easily intimidated are counseled "not to be more submissive than is becoming."[37] Gregory is aware of the proneness to self-deception amid seeming humility. The care of their souls requires helping them to see how they may be unnecessarily living out "a faulty timidity under the guise of humility."[38]

On the other hand, Gregory viewed persistent arrogance as having a primordially mysterious and transhistorical root in the demonic rebellion of the devil and his angels against the goodness of God because of their wish to be superior to God. This pattern was the mirror opposite of the redeemer who became as nothing in order to minister to humanity. "What, then, is baser than haughtiness, which, by overreaching itself, removes itself from the stature of true eminence? And what is more sublime than humility, which, in debasing itself to the lowest, joins itself to its Maker who remains above the highest?"[39]

The dynamics of arrogance have as much potential self-deception in them as do the dynamics of humility. Arrogance may firmly believe itself to be just while remaining quite ignorant of its own ploys. What is required pastorally in such a case? Gregory applies this analogy: The arrogant person is something like an unbroken horse, a wild, unruly animal that first must be stroked gently and only later controlled with aversive reinforcement. Pastoral care in this case is something like the treatment of a physician who provides a potent but distasteful drug to a highly resistant patient by mixing it with a generous amount of sweet honey. This is required for pastoral care of the arrogant, who otherwise would never take the medicine.[40]

Imagine an intensely egocentric individual who remains stubbornly resistant to all reasonable counsel. Ironically, such a person is more likely to change some behavior patterns if the amendment that is requested seems more a favor to someone else than a matter of self-profit. For self-centered persons judge everything in relation to its profit to themselves. If the pastor can initially convince the egocentric that the needed change is not for self-benefit but for the convenience of someone else, that is more likely to have greater appeal. The egocentric will quickly grasp that self-interest can then parade as altruism.

Gregory dutifully illustrates this with a Biblical type: When Hobab wanted to abandon the tribe of Israel and return to his home country, Moses had the practical problem of persuading him to continue in the covenant community; otherwise there would be no possibility of redemption. Moses, who already knew the way ahead, deliberately feigned an appeal to Hobab not to leave, citing as grounds the fact that Hobab knew the territory of the wilderness and could serve as the people's guide (Num. 10:29–31). The interaction is filled with irony: The self-centered man is being counseled by the wiser soul guide who already knows the way but who asks him anyway to be the leader, not because his leadership was necessary but in order that Hobab might be more profoundly led.[41]

The Fickle and the Obstinate

Some parishioners are prone to what Gregory calls "light-headedness." They are too easily influenced and therefore always changing their direction. Paul had recognized such persons in his congregations—people who were "whirled about by every fresh gust of teaching" (Eph. 4:14). Like Kierkegaard's aesthete, whose life is tyrannized by irresolution, such persons are always looking outside themselves to find a cure for their despair.

Their deeper dilemma, in Gregory's view, is that they tend to "undervalue and disregard themselves too much, and so are turned aside from their own judgment in successive moments of time."[42] When a whirlwind of opinion flies about them, they lose their identity because they refuse to choose, having never learned effectively to bind time with choice.

How is such a person to be dealt with pastorally? Gregory recognized that this individual is having difficulty in developing what we today would call increased ego strength and personal identity. Gregory's way of putting it carried the same meaning: It is as if one's soul or personal center is a leaf being blown around, so light that it does not have any substance. What one needs is, metaphorically speaking, an increased self-weight or heaviness, in the sense of a palpably defined selfhood as opposed to an identity lightness. When Gregory speaks here of "levity," he does not mean humor or wit, but technically a lack of substance to one's choosing and being, and therefore a lack of self-definition, self-understanding, and self-identity. So this person needs to be pastorally shepherded toward greater capacity for cutting through either/or decisions. If the central problem is irresolution which forever looks for someone else to give one direction, then the remedy is to grow in the capacity for decisive resolution. Gregory anticipates Kierkegaard's description of certain types of aesthetic nonchoosers who are habitually resistant to deciding anything.[43]

This pattern can be better grasped by comparison with its opposite, the assertive individualist, or as Gregory says, "The obstinate individual." There are people who overestimate their own capacity to make hard choices and who discount everybody else's judgment. Paul firmly counseled such characters to "be not wise in your own conceits" (Rom. 12:16, KJV). The conceit hinges on the fact that one cannot listen clearly to anyone else's view. One obstinately thinks that one's own opinion is weightier than anybody or everybody else's.

In this dipolar case study, Gregory enunciated a pivotal maxim that may be taken to be a major principle of his pastoral care: "certain faults beget others."[44] If you already have the fault of indecisiveness, you are therefore prone to becoming fickle. One fault begets another. If, on the other hand, you are already trapped in egocentric self-assertiveness, that is prone to beget obstinacy. Pastoral wisdom must grasp the difference between these two polarities, and wisely treat them in different ways. You do not want to cause the indecisive person to become even more weightless and pliable. You do not want to elicit in the assertive person greater obstinacy. What is needed is a finely tuned balance. Gregory sought to bring these virtues into an equilibrium so that neither exists in deficit or in excess.[45]

The Habitually Angry and the Meek

Returning to the emotive axis of interpersonal analysis, Gregory deals with two opposite types of pastoral challenges: the perennially outraged person and the excessively meek person.[46] How does the pastor wisely deal with the one who is always feeling offended, forever hankering for a fight? This is an interpersonal

posture that the classical tradition has termed "choleric"—
passionately angry, easily set off in confrontations, always ready
to be provoked and to provoke others, irascible, tending toward
malice and at times violence. All of these aggressive behaviors, as
we might guess, eagerly seek to parade outwardly as the laudable
virtues of justice, candor, and righteousness.[47]

Gregory was keenly aware of the complex psychological
dynamics of anger. One who perennially wants to fight may
unawarely be looking for someone to fight with. Thus there is a
tendency to provoke responses of anger and thereby to "succeed"
in eliciting aggression. Most persons would prefer not to have to
deal with the hazards of anger, but those of choleric temperament
may feel better when they are "hooking" or eliciting anger from
others, as it were, to test out their own strength. "The choleric
pursue even those who shun them, stirring up occasions of strife,
rejoicing in the trouble caused by contention."[48]

Gregory then takes the opposite case of the overly friendly
individual who does not have a developed capacity to confront
others. Such a person is intimidated by the slightest show of
hostility. Softened by the lack of ego-strength and critical capacity, this person is quickly immobilized by aggressive ploys, need-
ing to learn to express resistance more actively and assertively.

The wise counselor will search for a balanced equilibrim between conflict capability and the capacity for intimacy. Gregory's
unique way of pointing to this balance comes in his discussion of
the Holy Spirit, who combines these qualities in exemplary proportion. For the Holy Spirit is paradoxically symbolized by two
seemingly contrary symbols—dove and fire. Pastoral counsel
needs both. The wise counselor learns through dialogical experience to add to meekness zeal and to temper zeal with compassion.

Paul is Gregory's primary model of this equilibrium, especially
in Paul's exceptionally different vocational counsels to Timothy
and Titus.[49] To Timothy he said: Admonish others in all patience
(2 Tim. 4:2). To Titus he said: Admonish others with all authority
(Titus 2:15). Gregory thought that the difference of emphasis was

not accidental, but responsive to the varied predispositions of the two young men. His interpretation brings to a fitting conclusion this chapter on contextual pastoral counsel:

> Is it not that he sees Titus endowed with too meek a spirit, and Timothy with a little too zealous one? He enflames the one with zeal, and the other he restrains with a gentleness of patience. He gives to one what is lacking, he takes away from the other what is excessive. He aims at urging on the one with a spear; he checks the other with a bridle. Being the great husbandman that he is, having taken the church under his care, he waters some shoots that they may grow, but prunes others when he perceives their excessive growth.[50]

CHAPTER 4

Ironies
of Pastoral Counsel

As Gregory's dipolar method of pastoral case studies proceeds, each case seems to increase in complexity and deepen in pathos. The cases become more subtle and more heavily laden with irony as Gregory reveals the inner stresses of specific situations of counsel.

Although space limitations will not allow us to cover all these dipolarities, in this chapter we will select several prototype cases to examine in some detail. We are interested in revealing both Gregory's theological method of pastoral practice and the rudiments of his actual procedure of situational pastoral counsel.

Winners and Losers

Both life's winners and losers come to the pastor for help. Those who seem to live a charmed existence and to succeed in everything they do are to be pastorally guided in a direction that prevents them from becoming the victims of their own prosperity. They may need a gentle reminder that their success is not an unambiguous reward for virtue; rather, each new achievement stands as a challenge to learn to do good on that level of accomplishment or proficiency.[1]

Gregory thought that pastoral instruction to overachievers had already been anticipated by the Apostle Paul, who reminded his aggressive Corinthian flock that all historical achievements must be viewed eschatologically: "What I mean my friends is this. The time we live in will not last long. While it lasts, married men should be as if they had no wives; mourners should be as if they had nothing to grieve them, the joyful as if they did not rejoice; buyers must not count on keeping what they buy nor those who use the world's wealth on using it to the full. For the whole frame of this world is passing away" (1 Cor. 7:29–31). The point is not that persons should avoid buying or marrying or rejoicing but that each of these limited goods is to be viewed in relation to the source of all goods and received in due proportion, not be made absolute. If you buy something, live free from the illusion that you will always have possession of it. Use it "as if" you did not possess it, but only temporarily had stewardship of it. These are pertinent learnings for the person who is spoiled by success, who has not yet learned to deal with poverty or loss.[2]

A very different sort of pastoral counsel is needed, however, for those who have repeatedly made earnest attempts but never achieved their fondest goals. If they experience themselves always as losers, they may become wearied by the erosions of adversity. What sort of pastoral response is needed? They need most deeply to grasp that God has not given up on them. Two analogies apply: "When a physician gives up hope for a patient, he allows him to have whatever he fancies; but a person whose cure he deems possible is forbidden much that he desires. We take money away from our children yet at the same time reserve for them, as our heirs, the whole patrimony."[3] The ironic point for the loser is that if you are now suffering from adversity only then can you be certain that the Lord has not given up on you. The same point is powerfully made by Kierkegaard in his *Christian Discourses.*[4] The person who thinks himself a perennial loser needs the pastor's encouragement to be enabled to use those very circumstances of adversity for learning, spiritual growth, and discipline.

The Married and the Single

Those who think of marriage counseling as an exclusively modern phenomenon may be surprised to read that Gregory counsels those who are married to "study to please" their sexual partner.[5] Partners in marriage are above all counseled "to bear with mutual patience the things in which they sometimes displease each other"[6] (cf. Gal. 6:2). Gregory advises each marriage partner to think less on what one is forced to endure from one's spouse and more on what one's spouse is required to endure from oneself: "If one considers what is endured from one's self, that which is endured from another is more easily borne."[7]

Gregory's key to marriage counsel comes directly from Paul:

> The husband must give the wife what is due to her, and the wife equally must give the husband his due. The wife cannot claim her body as her own; it is her husband's. Equally the husband cannot claim his body as his own; it is his wife's. Do not deny yourselves to one another, except when you agree on a temporary abstinence (1 Cor. 7:3–5).

Marriage is not to be undertaken simply as a hedonic exercise to increase individual pleasure, without the sense of mutual accountability to one another, yet through this accountability the pleasing of one another is increased.[8]

Gregory strongly affirmed the freedom of the single state which he himself had chosen as a life-style. He does not share the often prevalent assumption that marriage is normative for mental health or necessary for the good life. He was convinced that the marital relationship involves the undertaking of an extraordinary responsibility that can potentially turn one away from God. Yet Gregory does not deprecate marriage, he even echoes Paul's dictum: "Better be married than burn with vain desire" (1 Cor. 7:9). Nonetheless, if one remains unmarried, one need not assume that one is psychologically incomplete or morally limited or spiritually incapacitated.

Suppose a parishioner is unmarried and yet has been involved in affairs, perhaps even deeply enmeshed and burned by relationships of intimacy, and is struggling with the guilt that so often comes from such entanglements. Gregory's pastoral counsel is hardly prudish. One should not assume that any sin is beyond the range of God, for "the life of one burning with love after having sinned is more pleasing to God than a life of innocence that grows languid in its sense of security."[9] Jesus made the same point sharply in his parable of the lost sheep: "I tell you there will be greater joy in heaven over one sinner who repents than over ninety-nine righteous people who do not need to repent" (Luke 15:7).

Gregory took special note of the woman who, having lived a wild life, brought oil of myrrh in a small flask, wetted Jesus' feet with tears, wiped them with her hair, kissed them, and annointed them with the myrrh. When the Pharisees said that he should reject this evil woman, Jesus said: "I tell you her great love proves that her many sins have been forgiven; when little has been forgiven, little love is shown" (Luke 7:36–50). The penitent adulterer is like land with thorns in it: "We love land that produces abundant fruit when its thorns are plowed in, more than land that has no thorns but which, though cultivated, yields a barren harvest."[10]

The Gluttonous and the Ascetic

Some eat to excess and others do not eat enough. Since the body is God's gift, to be properly cared for, eating enough but not too much is an appropriate concern of Christian counsel. The pastor from time to time will be called upon to give one kind of spiritual counsel to the gluttonous and another kind to the abstemious.[11]

You must not deal with both of these cases in the same way, Gregory warned. Paul realized that the abstemious may need to "use a little wine for thy stomach's sake, for thine often infirmities" (1 Tim. 5:23, KJV), whereas those more prone to gluttony may need to "abstain from meats" (1 Tim. 4:3 KJV). The pastor needs wisdom to know the difference between the former's need to relax constraints and the latter's need for disciplined self-constraint.

Gluttony is as much a spiritual as a bodily problem. Gregory's recurrent symbol for intemperate use of food is our first parents grabbing the forbidden fruit even when it was unmistakably prohibited. What do the gluttonous need? Although Gregory knew little about the physiology of heart disease, he grasped accurately the connection between long-term gluttony and the risk of sudden death. He quoted Jesus' injuction: "Keep a watch on yourselves; do not let your minds be dulled by dissipation and drunkenness and worldly cares so that the great Day closes upon you suddenly like a trap" (Luke 21:36).

Yet in the process of counseling persons in this direction one must carefully guard against the possibility that "in fleeing from the vice of gluttony worse vices are not generated."[12] Gluttony is not worse than the pride that may accompany its defeat.

He then turned to the opposite problem—excessive abstemiousness. Those who, perhaps out of some earnest motive, abstain too much from food may elicit new vices of excess, such as harshly judging others' motives. Paul rightly observed that the one who "does not eat must not pass judgment on the one who does" (Rom. 14:3). Like the Pharisees who boasted of fasting (Luke 18:12), the abstemious may be reinforcing egocentric pride over their abstinence.[13] Jesus warned that one is "not defiled by what goes into his mouth, but by what comes out of it" (Matt. 15:11).

The Protector and the Competitor

In any social organization there are some who are given responsibilities to care for and supply necessities to others, while others who are in a dependency position are called to receive what is given. The family is the most obvious example. Some give, some receive, each according to their capacity to give and receive. This principle of equity applies not only to parents of children, but also to leaders of any organization, administrators of any process, providers for any group. Some are charged with providing necessities for others. These persons can easily elicit anxiety or give offense and incur needless guilt if their ordering of resources is unwise, unjust, ill-conceived, or poorly administered.[14]

Gregory proceeds through a long list of the perennial problems of the givers and protectors, those whose social role is to provide care for others. They may be inclined toward moral conceit in which they "rate themselves above others on whom they bestow earthly goods."[15] They may be dilatory, through penuriousness or tightness inordinately delaying to give what is needed. They may give to some persons who rightly should not be given anything. They may give with an inordinate expectation of receiving thanks. They may give morosely so as to take away others' joy in receiving. Protectors and parent surrogates "must not esteem themselves to be better just because they see that others are supported by them."[16] The pastor will help them grasp that what they are dispensing actually belongs to others, and that it is truly just that the others should receive it. That the dependent receives goods is not a moral deficiency, nor is it a moral virtue to be in the role of dispenser.

If under the guise of liberality they "scatter uselessly what they have," pastoral counsel may need to focus more intently on the need for conservation of resources and for equitable distribution. But suppose the opposite is the case: they delay endlessly; they do not give enough. In this case Paul had to say that one who "sows sparingly will also reap sparingly" (2 Cor. 9:6, RSV). The benefactor is being called to give neither too much nor too little but to discover due proportion in giving a fit and equitable amount, responsive to the competing claims of ever-changing human needs.[17] If beneficence is accompanied by a moroseness that silently signals the recipient that it is a very heavy task indeed for the giver to provide, the touchstone of pastoral counsel is "God loves a cheerful giver" (2 Cor. 9:7, RSV).

The responsible protector, the person who is placed in the position of caring for others, is tempted in either of two directions—to give too little to one to whom something legitimately should be given, or to give too much to one who has less right to receive. In the former case the giver needs the injunction found in Luke 6:30: "Give to everyone who asks." In the latter case the person tempted to provide too liberally, even to those who have no legitimate needs, must be helped to realize that undue giving can reinforce dependency patterns.

Gregory makes a stunning point on the ambiguities of giving to those derelicts among the poor who are by consensus generally regarded as less worthy: One should give not just to the unworthy poor, but also to the worthy poor, regardless of their moral condition, and for a profound reason: because one "gives of his bread to an indigent sinner, not because he is a sinner, but because he is a man. In doing so one actually nourishes a righteous beggar, not a sinner, for he loves in him not his sin but his nature."[18]

Gregory sharply warned those with ample possessions not to imagine that they can put righteousness up for sale or sin with impunity while they deceive themselves into thinking that gifts to the poor will make up for their own sin. For he who "bestows food or raiment on the poor, yet is stained with wickedness in his soul or body, offers the lesser to righteousness and the greater to sin," for in giving to God his possessions he abandons his soul to death.[19]

An entirely different sort of pastoral counsel is appropriate for those acquisitive, competitive persons who are not looking after someone else's resources but trying only to acquire more resources for themselves. Gregory refers especially to those acquisitive people who tend toward opportunism or avarice, who are inclined to seize whatever they can at whatever cost to the other person in order to increase their own power or wealth or influence. Such tough, self-expansive, overly assertive persons may need to hear a tough-minded prognosis from scripture, which the pastor must find a way to say, as did the prophet Habakkuk: "Woe betide you who heap up wealth that is not yours and enrich yourself with goods taken in pledge! Will not your creditors suddenly start up, will not all awake who would shake you until you are empty, and will you not fall a victim to them?" (Hab. 2:6–7). Isaiah said straight out: "Shame on you! You who add house to house and join field to field, until not an acre remains, and you are left to deal alone in the land" (Isa. 5:8). The implication is that if you keep on expanding your power inordinately against the interest of others, then you may fail to see the hidden connection between your own interests and other persons' interests. Since you cannot learn to live with other people in this world, you may then have to experience painful loneliness as another sort of teacher. This is a damning correlation that the compulsively competitive person had better understand sooner rather than later. [20]

Like John Chrysostom before him, Gregory argued that one who "loves money can never have enough" (Eccl. 5:10). Avarice can never be really satisified.[21] The more the covetous invest their love in money, the more frustrated they will be in seeing that they will not be able to reap the fruit of happiness from it. One who makes haste to be rich will seldom be innocent (Prov. 28:20; 20:21). Jesus asked poignantly: "What is a man profited, if he shall gain the whole world, and lose his own soul?" (Matt. 16:26, KJV).

Gregory proposed a specific approach to the counsel of the compulsively withholding person who says: "I've done nothing wrong, I'm not hurting anybody. I'm just holding on to what I have." Such a person needs tactfully to be instructed that charity for the poor is not merely an act of mercy but also a matter of justice: "When we administer necessities to the needy, we give them what is their own, not what is ours, we pay a debt of justice, rather than do a work of mercy."[22] To the compulsive withholder Gregory retells the story of the barren fig tree: It did not harm anybody else, but it did in fact take up ground (Luke 13:7). The axe will be laid to such a tree, as John the Baptist remarked, if it does not produce fruit (Luke 3:9).

Sometimes lavish gifts are offered with a great show of outward rectitude. Gregory does not miss the opportunity to point out that the virtue of liberality may parade outwardly while it disguises the vice of avarice. Most pastors know parishioners who "carefully weigh what is the amount which they give, but neglect to consider how much they seize."[23] Gregory compared avarice with an overgrown plant that needs to be pruned. If you do not cut it regularly and carefully, it will grow unmanageably. The energies of self-assertive competition need to be curbed so that we may come to recognize the rights of others. Pastoral counsel seeks to do some of this timely pruning, reducing the tendency of avarice to grow wildly. The assumed joys of possession may become embittered by the poison of avarice. The avaricious cannot honestly "offer to God what they withdraw from the needy."[24] If you steal from the poor and offer stolen goods as a sacrifice to God, what is that like to God? It is like one who offers to sacrifice another man's son in the presence of his father (Sir. 34:20), an unendurable offense.

The Actively Guilty and the Passively Guilty

Those feeling guilt over willed misdeeds are treated differently than those who project fantasies of guilt beyond their willing. This important pastoral distinction is difficult to make and needs a general rule to guide its application. For those grieving over real guilt for actual misdeeds, Gregory hypothesizes that three stages are required for a return to moral health—penitence, pardon, and reparation. The pastoral intention must be to help keep the remorse or regret in due proportion to the values that have actually been negated.

It is appropriate that persons should first experience remorse and the struggle of conscience over unjust actions. The pastor must not try to protect persons from the witness of their own conscience and from going through a reasonable period of keen awareness of lost values.[25] During this process it is fitting that these losses should be felt before God and in the presence of God's holiness. The prototype of the penitential prayer is Psalm 51: "For I know my transgressions, and my sin is ever before me. Against thee, thee only, have I sinned" (vv. 3, 4, RSV). Pastoral listening cannot cheaply reduce the pain of standing before God in the remembrance of these losses.

But pastoral care does not end with moral sympathy; it continues, in the second place, with the proclamation of forgiveness, for the next pivotal movement of consciousness is the acceptance of divine pardon. Pastoral care, when effective, brings one articulately, clearly, and directly into the presence of divine mercy. The pastor must learn how to use human speech to declare the divine address. The aim is to assist the hearer in trusting God's forgiving Word and resting serenely in it. The parishioner who cannot meaningfully experience this deep dimension of forgiveness may fall into a habit that Gregory calls "immoderate affliction"[26]— forever overemphasizing one's deficits, always being too hard on oneself, seemingly making it impossible for God to forgive.

Pastoral care of the guilty proceeds, however, with still a third step that is not to be taken lightly—an appropriate act of reparation for wrongs done. Having once rested confidently in God's forgiveness, a new danger lurks, namely, that one will too readily assume that God will always forgive. This might tend to reinforce the temptation to do the same things over again, or worse. It would be to use God's pardon as an excuse for sinful self-assertion, turning God's unmerited mercy into "baneful reassurance."[27]

Yet every pastor knows that some people are inordinately burdened with guilt feelings. When these guilt feelings are carefully examined, they focus upon nothing that the individual has actually done but upon diffuse social guilt or felt corporate guilt, based on actions that were partially or wholly out of one's own hands. In some cases guilt adheres only to fantasized misdeeds that have been mentally conceived or imaginatively projected. Guilt in some cases is directed only to something one has thought of doing yet not actually done. Gregory would carefully guide such persons through a discriminating act of self-examination in order to sort out the degree of their own willingness to consent to a harmful deed. This exercise centers upon ascertaining the extent to which one would have given free consent to an overtly evil act had one been given full opportunity.

This self-examination is based on a clearly delineated psychology of will that Gregory had learned from earlier church fathers (Tertullian, Jerome, Augustine) but had himself developed and refined.[28] According to this psychology, the dynamics of guilt and self-alienation occur in three distinguishable stages, analogous to the fall of Adam. Stage one: A suggestion of sin is made. Stage two: one then thinks about the imagined pleasure that would accompany the misdeed. Stage three: one freely consents—one wills to do it. Even if one wills to punch a neighbor in the nose, however, one may still have to wait for the opportunity. Hence the crucial determination as to whether one has actually consented, stage three, may require deliberate and detailed self-examination.[29]

The psychological dynamics of this examination are further complicated by the fact that any of these three stages may be further enmeshed in a triadic collusion between (1) our flesh, which is aleady prone to sin, (2) a superpersonal demonic power, "the enemy," and (3) our own will, fully determined by us. In the last analysis it is only our will or spirit that can consent. Therefore only the will can sin. The body or flesh in itself has neither freedom or consent. By suggestion and temptation the demonic forces, Gregory hypothesized, were incessantly trying to lure the human will away from God. The flesh anticipates the imagined pleasure that might accompany a misdeed. Yet that in itself is not sin but only its precondition. At that point one may or may not give consent. It is the actual consent for which one is duly responsible. Parishioners are asked carefully to examine into which of these degrees of complicity they have fallen. The first and second degrees of complicity may carry some level of culpability, but finally one can sin only with one's own will. The psychological principle: the further one has actually gone toward freely willing a misdeed, the greater is the need for penitence, pardon, reparation, and reconciliation with God and neighbor.[30]

However far toward willing consent one may have gone, pastoral guidance nevertheless wishes to show that the divine pardon is immediately available to the truly penitent. The one who earnestly and actively prays for reconciliation can be confident that forgiveness is immediate and not delayed.[31]

Feigned Penitence and Penance
Without Restitution

Feigned penitent acts are in vain if they do not manifest themselves in seriously attempted behavioral changes. Bathing in tears
does not suffice. Gregory employs the devastating analogy of a
sow who, taking "a bath in its muddy wallow . . . makes itself even
filthier."[32] Those who pretend to be trying to change their behavior while pleading with God for forgiveness yet go right back to
the muddy wallow are opening themselves up to an even greater
deception—the mocking of God's pardon. The purpose of wash-
ing is to become clean. You may as well not take a bath in the first
place if you intend immediately to plunge back into the mud.
That amounts to thumbing one's nose at divine mercy.

Suppose you are called into court and plead with the judge for
pardon. You gain the pardon, walk right out of the court room,
and blatantly do again precisely the wrong for which you had
previously asked to be pardoned. Does that not show contempt of
the judge?[33] It is no easy matter to change such a steady disposi-
tion for evil. Those who are by strong predisposition morally evil
"are moved in vain by compunction to righteousness, just as, for
the most part, good are tempted to sin without harm."[34]

The pastor will meet those parshioners who will "Do some part
of a good deed without completing it,"[34] yet remain unduly confident that they have in fact done it already, and only when they will
find the regrettable side of their intention manifesting itself, will
they become naively surprised. Paul grasped the dynamics of this
inner dividedness in this memorable way: "In my inmost self I
delight in the law of God, but I perceive that there is in my bodily
parts a different law, fighting against the law which my reason
approves and makes me a prisoner under the law that is in my
members, the law of sin" (Rom. 7:22ff.). On this assumption, the
pastor does well to examine not only the initial expression of
regret over guilt, but beyond that whatever long-term behavior
patterns may follow after it. Gregory's analysis is largely consis-

tent with modern behavior modification theory and behavior therapy that focuses on actual, regularized, visible, even measurable, behavior change more than the hidden mysteries of supposed intentionality.[35]

Is reparation required? Gregory takes the case of a parishioner who, let us suppose, having at one point grossly sinned, has now completely desisted from that sin and yet does not wish to go through any semblance of an awkward or embarrassing act of penitence before God for past misdeeds. Inwardly the person is saying, "I'm not trapped there any more. Why do I need to repent?"

Gregory answers with three amusing analogies: a bad poem, an unpaid debt, and an unretrieved insult.[36] Suppose I write a very bad poem and then decide to give up writing. That does not efface what I have written just because I am not adding anything to it.

Suppose a person has gotten deeply into debt, but now has decided that he is not going to incur any more debts. That does not mean that all previous debts have been paid off. It simply means that no new debts are being incurred. The debtor still needs to pay off those old debts.

Suppose I insult you and then I say, "I am not going to insult you anymore." My being quiet does not make reparation for the earlier insult. I must go further than that.

Similarly, if it is God before whom we stand, "we certainly do not make reparation merely by ceasing from evil."[37] A further active step is needed—from penitence and pardon to the new life that emerges from it. One does not just undergo baptism and then do nothing, for baptism rehearses not only the death of an old life but also the rising to a new life.[38]

Those who frequently commit small misdeeds are to be counseled in a different way than those who sink into a grave sin only once in their life or very rarely. Frequent irresponsibilities are compared to tiny rain drops: if you get enough of them, they can cause a flood. It is something like a bee sting: one sting does not hurt much, but a thousand can destroy life as completely as a single rapier thrust to the heart. If bilge water is slowly and inconspicuously rising in a ship, and no one notices its continued rising, it has the same devastating effect as if a hurricane threw the ship on the rocks and dashed it to pieces. Thus, if you neglect these small incremental matters of behavioral deficit and minor excess, you may in time be lured into larger self-deceptions and collusions that will spell disaster.

This is the precise problem of the small misdeed—it fosters a lack of concern. One becomes inured to its consequences. One imagines that it is nothing at all. It is powerful only because it is small. Pastoral counsel will try to unpack the correlation between the raindrop and the impending flood, the bee sting and the death, the slowly rising water and the potential disaster.[39]

On the other side of the fence there is the individual who lives a solemnly upright life, whose small sins are carefully monitored, yet who suddenly finds himself in the midst of an unexpectedly grave sin. The prototype of this behavioral pattern is the legalist of whom Jesus wryly spoke, who filters his wine to get rid of a gnat, but then gulps down a camel (Matt. 23:24). Such persons discern trifles. They are clear about where the tiniest deficits lie. They tithe mint and cumin, the least of all of the herbs, yet forget the weightier matters of law, judgment, and mercy—and faith (Matt. 23:23). Overattentiveness to the small misdeed may contribute to the neglect of the large. To this is added pride, conceit, and a lethargy that comes from spiritual elation, an ecstatic awareness that assumes: "Aren't we wonderful!"[40]

The Nonstarter and the Nonfinisher

Gregory's next bipolar case study distinguishes between (1) one who never gets started on a good project, and (2) one who tends always to start things but never finish them. What pastor has not met both characters working together on the same committee!

The nonstarter must be pastorally assisted to see what values this syndrome is yielding and what it is losing. This may require a tough-minded pastoral encounter that penetrates pretense, absurdity, and immobility. One does not appeal verbally to the person merely to start doing something. You cannot plant until you first clear away weeds. "One who does not feel the pain of a wound will not seek any healing remedy."[41] The person who is infinitely tardy in getting started on an improved life-plan should be first shown the dire consequences that may ensue from the direction being pursued. Only then may one learn how good are the values one may now be disregarding.[42] On this basis a definite long-range plan may be pastorally commended. Gregory notes that the first act in construction of a house ironically may be an act of destruction—to cut down a tree. By analogy, the first step in getting started toward constructive change may be the painful negation of a dysfunctional pattern.

The case stands differently with those who never seem to complete any attempted good that they have begun. Here persistence is the soul of counsel: "The human soul is like a ship going up stream; it is not allowed to stay still in one place, because it will drop away to the lower reaches unless it strives to gain the upper."[43] The care of souls is like guiding a ship going up stream. The current is strong. One must work against the current all the time in order to make even the slightest progress. The instant you relax a step in your overall plan, you are already drifting downstream. This frustration must have been felt in the Church of Sardis to whom it was written: "Wake up, and put some strength into what is left, which must otherwise die! For I have not found any work of yours completed in the eyes of my God. So remember the teaching you received; observe it, and repent" (Rev. 3:1–3). This is not an unusual pastoral situation. The pastor is called to specifically teach persons how to complete what they have begun, so as not inadvertently to destroy hard-won goods that now exist but are vulnerable to erosion.[44]

An Especially Subtle Case

The secret evildoer and the anonymous do-gooder constitute the last pair of Gregory's bipolar cases. They present an especially subtle and intricate pastoral problem.

A unique pastoral task concerns the parishioner who inclines to do good openly while doing evil secretly.[45] Suppose you have a parishioner who has a wide public reputation for generosity, liberality, and mercy, yet secretly is doing something despicable. Such a person needs a special type and quality of pastoral admonition.

The most crucial learning to be sought in such a situation is the recognition of the fundamental difference between human judgments and divine judgment: that human achievements pass quickly while only the divine judgment is eternal and penetrates everything hidden. Ultimately, according to Gregory, each soul faces final divine judgment. All secret things will be revealed. The pastor does not do the parishioner a favor by withholding teaching about this final judgment. Jesus himself focused intently on this element in his pastoral care:

> Be careful not to make a show of your religion before men; if you do, no reward awaits you in your Father's house in heaven. Thus, when you do some act of charity, do not announce it with a flourish of trumpets, as the hypocrites do in synagogue and in the streets to win admiration from men. I tell you this: They have their reward already. No; when you do some act of charity, do not let your left hand know what your right is doing; your good deed must be secret, and your Father who sees what is done in secret will reward you" (Matt. 6:1–4).

The other side of this bipolar case study was for Gregory more complex, delicate, and intriguing. Suppose you have a parishioner who is prone to do good, but insists on doing that good in secret. Suppose this parishioner is even willing to allow another person openly to think badly of him or her so as to hide the good deed, deliberately concealing from everyone's view the good that has been done. Such a parishioner needs a very different kind of pastoral care than that given the secret evildoer. The anonymous benefactor is to be commended for taking seriously Jesus' teaching to avoid doing good works in order to be seen and approved by other people.

But it is possible that a good behavioral maxim may be carried too far. Gregory straightforwardly counseled such anonymous doers of good that they "should not love their neighbors less than themselves"![46] If in every case you withhold edification from others by concealing the good you do, then nobody else can ever possibly enjoy, emulate, or benefit from that good work. This is why Jesus proclaimed:

> You are light for all the world. A town that stands on a hill cannot be hidden. When a lamp is lit, it is not put under the meal-tub, but on the lamp-stand, where it gives light to everyone in the house. And you, like the lamp, must shed light among your fellows, so that, when they see the good that you do, they may give praise to your Father in heaven (Matt. 5:14–16).

But how can it be consistently said on the one hand that we should allow other persons to see our good works (Matt. 5:16), and on the other hand that we should take heed that we do not do our good works in order to be seen by others (Matt. 6:1)? Gregory thinks that these two admonitions, properly understood, are not inconsistent: We are called to do good not in such a way as to be seen by others with a view to drawing to ourselves their praise, but in a way that allows others to see God's love and constant mercy refracted through our behavior.[47] The key difference lies not in the realm of outward activity, but in the realm of inward motivation. It makes sense that, as we do outward good works, others be allowed to behold something of our inner motives for doing them, and of the positive effect of our hidden good motives— though the good deed is not to be done primarily in order to be outwardly observed by others. When others nonetheless behold our good deed, done openly, not for our own glory but for the well-being of our neighbor and the glory of God, they can then receive it, celebrate it, and imitate it. In this sense, good deeds should not be concealed, and, except in rare cases, persons should not carelessly allow evil to be attributed to them. Gregory argued that such persons have some responsibility even for the way others interpret their behavior. Why? Because every person's behavior is at some level exemplary. Others may imitate what they perceive to be your behavior, even if they are inaccurate in their perception of it.[48]

Gregory's biblical prototype for thinking about this pastoral admonition is again Paul. In Corinth the question had arisen concerning the eating of food consecrated to heathen deities. Paul's most eager hearers were saying, "Forget dietary rules. These are false gods." Paul agreed, yet added:

> But not everyone knows this. There are some who have been so accustomed to heathen consecration, and their conscience, being weak, is polluted by the eating. Certainly food will not bring us into God's presence: If we do not eat, we are none the worse, and if we eat, we are none the better. But be careful that this liberty of yours does not become a pitfall for the weak. If a weak character sees you sitting down to a meal in a heathen temple—you who 'have knowledge'—will not his conscience be emboldened to eat food consecrated to the heathen diety? This 'knowledge' of yours is utter disaster to the weak, the brother for whom Christ died. In thus sinning against your brothers and wounding their conscience, you sin against Christ" (1 Corinthians 8).

In this way parishioners are counseled to be responsible, not only for their own actual behavior, but also for the way that behavior is perceived by others. Even if we are doing something good, others with weak conscience might perceive it as a stumbling block, the means of another's downfall: in that case we are in some sense partly responsible for that stumbling.

Gregory summarizes his response to these two dipolar cases with this concise maxim: The pastor will help parishioners learn to do good deeds *secretly* insofar as they are motivated by the need for praise, but *openly* insofar as they become a means of the glorification of God and the edification of the neighbor.[49]

Conclusion:
Preaching and
Pastoral Care

Gregory's *Pastoral Care* is the most influential book in the history of the pastoral tradition. In it he deals discretely with highly individualized remedies. Pastoral wisdom must listen intently to the unique characteristics of a situation and apply a specific remedy accordingly.

When dealing with a community of hearers, however, rather than counseling in one-on-one dialogue, the task of pastoral care becomes infinitely more volatile and hazardous. For in preaching, the pastor must deal simultaneously with persons of widely different needs, ploys, and passions.

To what degree can pastoral care meaningfully occur through preaching? Gregory's basic maxim is still a useful guide, even though difficult to apply: An exhortation that is intended to be delivered to a general audience must be gauged in such a way that "virtues are fostered in each without encouraging the growth of vices opposed to such virtues."[1] This requires exceptional skill and preparation on the part of the speaker. Preachers must be aware of the diversity of persons in their congregation, yet try to speak so that the Spirit, through scripture, addresses many hearts in ways that will be fitting to each, as different as these hearers are known to be from one another.

In the last poignant section of his *Pastoral Care* Gregory provides a pithy summary of the complex balance needed to foster virtue without inadvertently encouraging vice. That section is worth reading, carefully and meditatively. It is reviewed as a concise and fitting summary to our lengthy expedition.

> Humility is to be preached to the proud in a way not to increase fear in the timorous, and confidence infused into the timorous, as not to encourage the unbridled impetuosity in the proud. The idle and the remiss are to be exhorted to zeal for good deeds, but in a way not to increase the unrestraint of intemperate action in the impetuous. Moderation is to be imposed on the impetuous without producing a sense of listless security in the idle. Anger is to be banished from the impatient, but so as not to add to the carelessness of the remiss and easy-going. The remiss should be fired with zeal in such a manner as not to set the wrathful ablaze."[2]

Such preaching prays to be enlivened by the Spirit that it may reach its precise targets.

Indeed pastoral care can and must be attempted through preaching: "Good things are so to be preached as not to give incidental help to what is bad."[3] More than fleshly wisdom or human cleverness is required if one is to encourage a balance of behavioral excellences without eliciting new behavioral deficits. Gregory's dialectical balance is exquisite: "The highest good is to be so praised that the good in little things is not discarded. Attention should be called to the little things, but not in such a way that they are deemed sufficient and there is no striving for the highest."[4]

The pastor in public communication continues to care for souls publicly but within a communication context that differs from that of individual dialogue. The problem of pastoral preaching becomes even more complicated when you realize that any one of those hearers may experience inwardly contrary passions at any given time. This makes the public task of care of souls through preaching challenging and exacting. Gregory compares pastoral preaching to an act of wrestling—deftly dodging quickly this move and that ploy while trying to get in a telling move at exactly the right time.[5]

Gregory's idea of pastoral preaching hinges on his notion of

contrary compulsions. The hearer who is temperamentally op-
timistic and ordinarily self-affirming will at certain times become
deeply depressed, overwhelmed with sadness. The pastor's problem in public communication is to offer encouragement that takes
into account the pain yet will not link easily with false optimism.

The plot thickens, however, when the pastoral preacher
realizes that other parishioners sitting in the same congregation
have their own distinctive sets of ambivalent tendencies and passions. Such individuals may be plagued with inordinate hastiness,
always running around with high anxiety levels; yet on certain
occasions, when they need to do something quickly, they may be
suddenly gripped by fear. The pastoral preacher tries to assist the
person suffering from those two distinguishable psychological
syndromes—which Gregory terms precipitancy and anxiety. The
pastor hopes that the hurriedness can be diminished, but without
thereby intensifying the anxieties. In speaking with such a pre-
cipitously anxious person, the pastor is also aware of the self-
affirming optimist in the next pew, who suffers from an entirely
different set of contrary compulsions.

In confronting this perennial problem in the care of souls
Gregory again turns to a medical analogy: Sometimes a person
who has a constitutionally weak body experiences a violent illness
that requires a drastic remedy. If the body cannot endure the
strong remedy, the doctor must treat the violent illness in such a
way that the fatigue and weakness of the body is not increased.
This may require the application of treatments that are ironically
working in opposite directions. You are trying both to counteract
the violent illness and the fatigue at one and the same time—in
due proportion, as the body is able to take on two different, even
countermanding, treatments. This is the hazardous ground over
which the care of souls must at times warily proceed. When a
person suffers from distinctly contrary compulsions, the care
given may be analogous to that involved in giving highly refined
doses of medication. It calls for a subtle timing sequence that can
help the person actually take one administrable treatment in due

course while delaying another unadministrable treatment in hopes that the conflicting treatments do not become worse than the illness itself.[6]

It is for this reason that sometimes a smaller compulsion may be temporarily disregarded in order that the greater and more dangerous compulsion can be pastorally treated. Suppose an individual has two major contrary compulsions, one of which is mildly dangerous, and the other of which is gravely dangerous. Would not pastors then be justified in allowing the lesser problem to increase if, in doing so, they are able to work significantly on the more severe compulsion that conceivably could cause something worse?

It is not unusual therefore to find pastoral care "overlooking what was mildly wrong," in order to take seriously what matters more urgently.[7] Effective pastoral care must be free to exercise a kind of tolerance for vice, allowing a certain compulsion to continue while deliberately reducing another more dangerous one.[8]

Should pastors always tell a person the whole truth, or should they withhold the truth at times when it cannot possibly be assimilated? Gregory argues that the application of truth in pastoral situations must be explicitly gauged to the capacity of the hearer to grasp the truth; otherwise the truth can be dangerously ill-timed. He compares the pastor's approach in this connection to the string of a violin that must be tuned to exactly the right pitch. Too loose, the string sounds flat; too tight, it may snap. There is a danger in offering to weak and unprepared souls the most profound truth at the wrong time. Such was the dilemma that caused Paul to write to the congregation at Corinth: "For my part, my brothers, I could not speak to you as I should speak to people who have the Spirit. I had to deal with you on the merely natural plane, as infants in Christ. And so I gave you milk to drink, instead of solid food, for which you were not ready" (1 Cor. 3:1–2).

Gregory thought that the pastor is responsible for even inadvertent use of language. By negligence, the pastor remains responsible for things said inaccurately or accidently. "When a man removes the cover of a well or digs a well and leaves it uncovered, then if an ox or an ass falls into it, the owner of the well shall make good the loss" (Exod. 21:33). Similarly, if we are negligent in speech, if we leave behind us a hazardous, uncovered well, then if someone falls in and is injured, we are responsible. Where one's footsteps go is a truer indication than where one's words go. Rather than relying exclusively upon words, as if they were in themselves the sole agency of pastoral care, it is better to view one's deeds as basic proclamation. Inevitably the parishioner will see through language to its actual correspondence with behavior.

The seriousness with which Gregory himself took this maxim is revealed in the concluding comment of his *Pastoral Care,* where he sighs:

> I, miserable painter that I am, have painted a portrait of an ideal man; and here I have been directing others to the shore of perfection, I, who am still tossed about on the waves of sin. But in the shipwreck of this life, sustain me I beseech you, with the plank of your prayers, so that, as my weight is sinking me down, you may uplift me with your meritorious hand.[9]

Notes

PREFACE

1. The twentieth century has produced only one English edition of Gregory. The number of early imprints in the history of printing is a fair indication of the immense popularity of Gregory's *Pastoral Care* in the late medieval period. In the thirty years after the publication of its first edition in 1471 there were seven editions in Latin alone. They were followed by six more editions in the sixteenth century.

INTRODUCTION

1. This theme eventually became the core of the argument of my *Kerygma and Counseling* (Philadelphia: Westminster Press, 1966; San Francisco: Harper & Row, 1978). I sought at that time to show how the same hypothesis could be related to Freudian, Adlerian, and Gestalt approaches to psychotherapy. At the time I was teaching pastoral counseling and theology, and guiding a general hospital pastoral education program.

2. For the results of this period of research, see my *Contemporary Theology and Psychotherapy* (Philadelphia: Westminster Press, 1967), and *The Structure of Awareness* (Nashville: Abingdon Press, 1969).

3. See my *The Intensive Group Experience* (Philadelphia: Westminster Press, 1972).

4. See my *Game Free: The Meaning of Intimacy* (New York: Harper & Row, 1974).

5. This shift was first publicly expressed in *After Therapy What?* 1972 Finch Lectures, Fuller School of Psychology, with responses by N. Warren, K. Mulholland, C. Schoonhoven, C. Kraft, and W. Walker (Springfield, Ill: Charles C. Thomas, 1974).

6. See my *TAG: The Transactional Awareness Game* (New York: Harper & Row, 1976).

7. See my *Should Treatment Be Terminated?* (San Francisco: Harper & Row, 1976).

8. See Søren Kierkegaard, *Parables of Kierkegaard*, ed. Thomas C. Oden (Princeton: Princeton University Press, 1978).

9. See my *Agenda for Theology: Recovering Christian Roots* (San Francisco: Harper & Row, 1979).

CHAPTER 1

1. For a more complete bibliography of the classics of the pastoral tradition, please refer to the 1200 or so entries in the bibliography of my *Pastoral Theology: Essentials of Ministry* (San Francisco: Harper & Row, 1983), 317–54. Regrettably a large number of these books are out of print. Our purpose in setting forth this modest preliminary list is to help the reader to become aware that there is in fact a definite body of important pastoral texts once widely known but now largely neglected.

2. Erik Erikson, *Identity and the Life Cycle* (New York: International Universities Press, 1959), chaps. 2,3.

3. William G. T. Shedd, *Homiletics and Pastoral Theology* (New York: Charles Scribner's Sons, 1867).

4. Patrick Fairbairn, *Pastoral Theology* (Edinburgh: T. & T. Clark, 1872).

5. James M. Hoppin, *Pastoral Theology* (New York: Funk & Wagnalls, 1884).

6. Charles Bridges, *The Christian Ministry* (New York: Robert Carter, 1847).

7. Heinrich Koestlin, *Die Lehre von der Seelsorge* (Berlin: Reuther and Reichard, 1895).

8. Washington Gladden, *The Christian Pastor* (New York: Charles Scribner's Sons, 1898).

9. Daniel Kidder, *The Christian Pastorate* (New York: Methodist Book Concern, 1871).

10. Seward Hiltner, *Pastoral Counseling* (Nashville: Abingdon Press, 1949); Howard Clinebell, *Basic Types of Pastoral Counseling* (Nashville: Abingdon Press, 1966); Wayne E. Oates, *Pastoral Counseling* (Philadelphia: Westminster Press, 1974); and Carroll A. Wise, *Pastoral Counseling* (New York: Harper & Bros., 1951).

11. Dietrich Stollberg, *Therapeutische Seelsorge* (Munich: Chr. Kaiser, 1969); Paul Tournier, *The Doctor's Casebook in the Light of the Bible* (New York: Harper and Bros., 1960); Joseph Nuttin, *Psychoanalysis and Personality* (New York: New American Library, 1962).

12. Anton Boisen, *Out of the Depths* (New York: Harper & Bros., 1960).

13. This history has been partially chronicled in Seward Hiltner, ed., *Clinical Pastoral Training* (New York: Federal Council of Churches, 1945); Charles Kemp, *Physicians of the Soul: A History of Pastoral Counseling* (New York: Macmillan Co. 1947); Edward Thornton, *Professional Education for Ministry: A History of Clinical Pastoral Education* (Nashville: Abingdon Press, 1969).

14. Frank Lake, *Clinical Theology* (London: Darton, Longman & Todd, 1966).

15. Paul Vitz, *Psychology As Religion* (Grand Rapids: Wm. B. Eerdmans, 1977).

16. For a general review of these therapeutic effectiveness studies, see my articles, "A Populist's View of Psychotherapeutic Deprofessionalization," *Journal of Humanistic Psychology*, (Spring 1974) and "Consumer Interests in Therapeutic Outcome Studies," *Journal of Humanistic Psychology* 15 (Summer 1975), as well as *Game Free*, chap. 3.

17. See *The Intensive Group Experience*, chaps. 1, 5.

18. See chap. 1 of my discussion in *Guilt Free* (Nashville: Abingdon Press, 1980).

19. Karl Menninger, *Whatever Became of Sin?* (New York: Hawthorn Books, 1972); Lake, *Clinical Theology*; Paul Pruyser, *The Minister as Diagnostician* (Philadelphia: Westminster Press, 1976); O. Hobart Mowrer, *The Crisis in Psychiatry and Religion* (New York: Van Nostrand, 1961); Ruth Barnhouse, "Spiritual Direction and Psychotherapy," *Journal of Pastoral Care* 33 (September 1979): 149–63; Vitz, *Psychology as Religion*.

20. Pruyser, *Minister as Diagnostician*, 39f.

21. Gilbert Burnet, *A Discourse of the Pastoral Care*, 1692 (London: W. Baynes, 1818); Jacob Sailer, *Vorlseungen aus der Pastoraltheologie* (Munich: J. J. Lentner, 1788).

22. Cf. Dietrich Bonhoeffer, *Letters and Papers from Prison* (New York: Macmillan Co., 1953).

23. Cf. my *Contemporary Theology and Psychotherapy*, 62–64.

CHAPTER 2

1. Frederick Homes Dudden, *Gregory the Great* (London: Longmans, Green, and Co., 1905), 1: chaps. 1, 2.

2. James Barmby, *Gregory the Great* (New York: Pott, Young & Co., 1879), chap. 1.

3. Dudden, *Gregory the Great*, 1: 31ff.

4. Gregory the Great, *Morals on the Book of Job*, 3 vols., trans. J. Bliss,

Library of the Fathers of the Holy Catholic Church Series (Oxford: John Henry Parker, 1850).

5. Henry Hoyle Howorth, *Saint Gregory the Great* (London: J. Murray, 1912).

6. Pierre Batiffol, *Saint Gregory the Great*, trans. John L. Stoddard (London: Burns, Oates & Washbourne, 1929), chaps. 1, 2.

7. Barmby, *Gregory the Great*.

8. Gregory the Great, *The Book of Pastoral Rule* (hereafter noted as *BPR*), and *Epistles*, Nicene and Post-Nicene Fathers (hereafter NPNF), 2d series, vol. 12 (Grand Rapids: Wm. B. Eerdmans, 1976), *Epistles*, chaps. 5, 18.

9. Dudden, *Gregory the Great*, 2 passim.

10. *BPR, Epistles* 1.40, 1.56, 7.38, 10.7.

11. Howorth, *Saint Gregory*, passim.

12. Gregory the Great, *Dialogues*, Fathers of the Church series, vol. 39 (New York: Catholic University Press, n.d.).

13. Gregory the Great, *Pastoral Care*, trans. Henry Davis, Ancient Christian Writers series, vol. 11 (Westminster, Md.: Newman, 1950), hereafter noted as *PC*. The reference here is to *PC* 3.20.

14. Ibid., 2.9.

15. Ibid., 2.7.

16. *BPR* 2.6.

17. Cf. Oden, *Kerygma and Counseling*, chap. 1.

18. Joseph Wolpe, *The Practice of Behavior Therapy* (New York: Pergamon Press, 1969); *PC* 3.3.

19. Sigmund Freud, *Complete Psychological Works*, Standard Ed. (London: Hogarth, 1953–), 14: 17.

20. Carl G. Jung, *Collected Works* (Princeton: Princeton University Press, 1959–).

21. A. Mehrabian, *Nonverbal Communication* (Chicago: Aldine Publishing, 1972); Alexander Lowen, *Betrayal of the Body* (New York: Macmillan Co., 1967).

22. Carl R. Rogers, *On Becoming a Person* (Boston: Houghton Mifflin, 1961).

23. *PC* 2.1.

24. Ibid.

25. *BPR* 2.1.

26. *PC* 1.1.

27. Ibid., 1.2.

28. Ibid.

29. *BPR* 1.2.
30. Ibid.
31. *PC* 1.1–3.
32. Ibid., 1.2–3.
33. Ibid., 1.3.
34. Ibid., 1.4.
35. Ibid., 2.5.
36. *BPR* 1.5.
37. *PC* 1.5,6.
38. Ibid., 1.6.
39. Ibid., 1.7.
40. Ibid.
41. Ibid., 1.8.
42. Ibid., 1.9.
43. Ibid., 1, 10.
44. Ibid., 1.10,11.
45. Ibid., 1.11.
46. *BPR* 2.2.
47. *PC* 2.3.
48. *BPR* 2.3.
49. *PC* 2.4.
50. *BPR* 2.5.
51. *PC* 2.5.
52. Ibid., 2.4.
53. Ibid., 2.6.
54. Cf. ibid., 2.6.
55. Ibid.
56. *BPR* 2.6.
57. *PC* 2.6.
58. Ibid.
59. Ibid.
60. *BPR* 2.6.
61. Ibid.
62. *PC* 2.6.
63. *BPR* 2.7.
64. *PC* 2.8.
65. Ibid.
66. Ibid., 2.10.
67. Ibid.
68. Ibid.

69. Ibid.
70. Ibid.

CHAPTER 3

1. *PC* 3, Prologue.
2. Gregory of Nazianzus, *Orations and Letters*, NPNF, 2d series, vol. 7 (Grand Rapids: Wm. B. Eerdmans, 1976) "Second Oration," 210ff.
3. *PC* 3, Prologue.
4. Ibid., 3.1.
5. Cf. Oden, *TAG*, 3–26.
6. *PC* 3.7.
7. Ibid.
8.. *PC* 3.8.
9. *BPR* 2.8.
10. *PC* 3.9.
11. Ibid.
12. Ibid.
13. *BPR* 3.9.
14. *PC* 3.9.
15. Ibid.
16. Ibid.
17. For a fuller bibliography of this literature, see my *TAG*, 116ff.
18. Oden, *TAG*, 1–17.
19. *PC* 3.22.
20. Ibid.
21. Ibid.
22. *PC* 3.23.
23. *BPR* 3.22.
24. Ibid.
25. Ibid.
26. Oden, *TAG*, 3–10.
27. *PC* 3.4.
28. Ibid.
29. Ibid.
30. *PC* 3.5.
31. *PC* 3.2.
32. Ibid.
33. Ibid.
34. *BPR* 3.2.

35. *PC* 3.2.
36. *PC* 3.17.
37. Ibid.
38. Ibid.
39. Ibid.
40. Ibid.
41. Ibid.
42. *PC* 3.18.
43. Ibid.
44. Ibid.
45. Ibid.; cf. 2.2ff.
46. *PC* 3.16; cf. Oden, *TAG*, 3ff.
47. *PC* 3.16; cf. Erving Goffman, *The Presentation of the Self in Everyday Life* (Garden City, N.Y.: Doubleday & Co., 1959).
48.. *PC* 3.16.
49. Ibid.
50. Ibid.

CHAPTER 4

1. *PC* 3.26.
2. Ibid.
3. Ibid.
4. Søren Kierkegaard, *Christian Discourses* (New York: Oxford University Press, 1940).
5. *PC* 2.27.
6. *PC* 3.27.
7. Ibid.
8. Cf. Søren Kierkegaard, *Either/Or* (Princeton: Princteon University Press, 1971), vol. 2.
9. *BPR* 3.2.
10. *PC* 3.28.
11. *PC* 3.19.
12. Ibid.
13. *BPR* 3.19.
14. *PC* 3.20.
15. Ibid.
16. Ibid.
17. Ibid.
18. *BPR* 3.20.
19. *PC* 3.20.

20. Ibid.
21. Ibid.; cf. John Chrysostom, *Homilies on the Acts,* NPNF, 1st series, vol. 9.
22. *PC* 3.21.
23. Ibid.
24. Ibid.
25. *PC* 3.29.
26. Ibid.
27. Ibid.
28. Ibid.; cf. Tertullian, *On Penitence,* Ante-Nicene Fathers, vol. 3, (Grand Rapids: Wm. B. Eerdmans, 1976); Jerome, NPNF, 2d series, vol. 6; Augustine, *Confessions and Enchiridion,* Library of Christian Classics, vol. 7 (Philadelphia: Westminster Press, 1953).
29. *PC* 3.29.
30. Ibid.
31. Ibid.
32. *PC* 3.30.
33. Ibid.
34. Ibid.
35. *BPR* 3.30.
36. *PC* 3.30.
37. Ibid.
38. Ibid.
39. *BPR* 3.30.
40. *PC* 3.30.
41. *PC* 3.34.
42. Ibid.
43. Ibid.
44. Ibid.
45. *PC* 3.35.
46. Ibid.
47. Ibid.
48. *BPR* 3.35.
49. *PC* 3.35.

CONCLUSION

1. *PC* 3.36.
2. Ibid.
3. Ibid.
4. Ibid.

5. Ibid.
6. *PC* 3.37.
7. *PC* 3.38.
8. Ibid.
9. Ibid.